This volume presents new versions of key chapters from the recent Routledge/Open University textbook, *Creative Writing: A Workbook with Readings* for writers who are specialising in writing poetry. It offers the novice writer engaging and creative activities, making use of insightful, relevant readings from the work of well-known authors to illustrate the techniques presented.

Using his experience and expertise as a teacher as well as a poet, Bill Herbert guides aspiring writers through such key writing skills as:

- drafting
- voice
- imagery
- rhyme
- form
- theme.

The volume is further updated to include never-before published dialogues with prominent poets such as Vicki Feaver, Gillian Allnutt, Kathleen Jamie, Linda France, Douglas Dunn, Sean O'Brien and Jo Shapcott. Concise and practical, *Writing Poetry* offers an inspirational guide to the methods and techniques of this challenging and rewarding genre and is a must-read for aspiring poets.

W. N. Herbert is Professor of Poetry and Creative Writing at Newcastle University. He has published seven volumes of poetry and four pamphlets. His poetry has won a variety of awards and accolades.

RELATED TITLES FROM ROUTLEDGE AND THE OPEN UNIVERSITY

Life Writing
Sarah Haslam and Derek Neale

This practical guide covers key life writing skills including writing what you know, biography and autobiography, prefaces, form, memory, characters, and novelistic, poetic and dramatic techniques. *Life Writing* presents never-before published interviews with successful life writers such as Jenny Diski, Robert Fraser, Richard Holmes, Michael Holroyd, Jackie Kay, Hanif Kureishi and Blake Morrison.

ISBN13: 978–0–415–46153–5 (pbk)

Writing Fiction
Linda Anderson and Derek Neale

This useful volume guides aspiring writers through crucial aspects of their craft, outlining how to stimulate creativity, keeping a writer's notebook, character creation, setting, point of view, structure and showing and telling. *Writing Fiction* includes never-before published interviews with writers such as Andrew Cowan, Stevie Davies, Maggie Gee, Andrew Greig and Hanif Kureishi.

ISBN13: 978–0–415–46155–9 (pbk)

Available at all good bookshops
For ordering and further information please visit:
www.routledgeliterature.com

Writing Poetry

W. N. Herbert

Routledge
Taylor & Francis Group

LONDON AND NEW YORK

First edition published 2010
by Routledge
2 Park Square, Milton Park, Abingdon, Oxon, OX14 4RN

Simultaneously published in the USA and Canada
by Routledge
270 Madison Avenue, New York, NY 10016

Routledge is an imprint of the Taylor & Francis Group, an informa business

© 2010 The Open University

Typeset in Frutiger and Times by RefineCatch Limited, Bungay, Suffolk
Printed and bound in Great Britain by CPI Antony Rowe, Chippenham, Wiltshire

British Library Cataloguing in Publication Data
A catalogue record for this book is available from the British Library

Library of Congress Cataloging in Publication Data
A catalog record for this book has been requested

ISBN13: 978–0–415–46154–2
ISBN10: 0–415–46154–5

Contents

Acknowledgements

The publisher and author would like to thank the following for permission to reprint material under copyright:

'A Free Translation' by Craig Raine, © Craig Raine 1984. By permission of the author care of DGA Ltd.

'The Cupboard' from *The Tree House* by Kathleen Jamie, © 2004. Used by permission of Pan Macmillan Publishers Ltd, London.

'Cousin Coat', 'At the Well Gate' and 'The Provincial Station' from *Cousin Coat: Selected Poems 1976–2001* by Sean O'Brien, © 2002. Used by permission of Pan Macmillan Publishers Ltd, London.

'Age of Anxiety' by W.H. Auden, from *Collected Longer Poems*, © 1968. By permission of Faber and Faber Ltd.

'You', 'Extra Helpings', 'Loch Music' by Douglas Dunn, from *New Selected Poems*, © 2003. By permission of Faber and Faber Ltd.

'Quoof' by Paul Muldoon, from *Quoof*, © 2001. By permission of Faber and Faber Ltd.

'The Mad Cow Talks Back', 'Goat', 'Rosa Gallica', 'Rosa Hemispherica', 'Rosa Sancta' by Jo Shapcott, from *Tender Taxes*, © 2001. By permission of Faber and Faber Ltd.

'Sherdi' by Sujata Bhatt, from *Point no Point*, © 1997. By permission of Carcanet Press Ltd.

'Cooking with Blood', 'Trying to Explain Telescope' by Linda France, from *The Simultaneous Dress* (Tarset: Bloodaxe, 2002). By permission of the author.

'Body Language' by Linda France, from *The Gentleness of the Very Tall* (Newcastle: Bloodaxe, 1994). By permission of the author.

'The Axolotl' by Ogden Nash, originally published in the *New Yorker* (1957). Copyright © 1957 by Ogden Nash. Reprinted by permission of Curtis Brown, Ltd.

'Strange Meeting' by Wilfred Owen. From *Wilfred Owen: The War Poems* ed. by Jon Stalworthy (London: Chatto and Windus, 1994). By permission of Jon Stalworthy.

'Glasgow Sonnets' by Edwin Morgan from *Collected Poems* © 1990. By permission of Carcanet Press Ltd.

'Johann Joachim Quantz's Five Lessons' by W.S. Graham, from *New Collected Poems* © 2004. By permission of Michael and Margaret Snow.

'The Silk Light of Advent', 'Child', 'Dottle, Donkey Man', 'My Camberwell Grandmother Before her Marriage' by Gillian Allnutt from *How the Bicycle Shone: New & Selected Poems* © 2007. Used by permission of Bloodaxe Books Ltd.

'Portrait of My Lover as a Strange Animal' by Selima Hill from *Gloria: Selected Poems* © 2007. Used by permission of Bloodaxe Books Ltd.

'Mr & Mrs Scotland are Dead' by Kathleen Jamie from *Mr & Mrs Scotland are Dead: Poems 1980–1994,* © 2002. Used by permission of Bloodaxe Books Ltd.

'Maiden Speech' by Eleanor Brown from *Maiden Speech* © 1996. Used by permission of Bloodaxe Books Ltd.

'The Shrimp' by Ogden Nash from *Candy is Dandy: The Best of Ogden Nash* by Ogden Nash with an introduction by Anthony Burgess, © 1994. Reprinted by permission of The Carleton Publishing Group Limited.

'Summer Farm' by Norman MacCaig from *The Poems of Norman MacCaig*, © 2005. Used by permission of Birlinn Ltd, Edinburgh.

'Dreaming Frankenstein' in *Dreaming Frankenstein & Collected Poems* by Liz Lochead © 1984. Used by permission of Birlinn Ltd, Edinburgh.

'The Man who Ate Stones', and 'The Gun' from *The Book of Blood* © 2006. 'The Handless Maiden' from *The Handless Maiden* © 1994 by Vicki Feaver, published by Jonathan Cape © 1994. Used by permission of the Random House Group Ltd.

'Leaving Innismore' by Michael Longley, from *Selected Poems of Michael Longley*, published by Jonathan Cape, © 1998. Reprinted by Permission of the Random House Group.

'A Peculiar Suicide' from *SELECTED POEMS* by Matthew Sweeney, published by Jonathan Cape, © 1992. Reprinted by Permission of The Random House Group Ltd.

'No. 233' (3 lines) from *ON LOVE AND BARLEY: HAIKU OF BASHO* by Basho, translated and with an introduction by Lucien Stryk (Penguin Classics, 1985). Copyright © Lucien Stryk, 1985. Reproduced by permission of Penguin Books Ltd.

'Ode to Salt' from *The Selected Odes of Pablo Neruda* by Pablo Neruda, translated by Margaret Sayers Peden, © 1990 Fundacion Pablo Neruda. Published by the University of California Press.

'Bamboo Grove House' (p.31) (4 lines) from *WEI WANG: POEMS* translated with an introduction by G.W. Robinson (Penguin Classics, 1973). Copyright © G.W. Robinson, 1973. Reproduced by permission of Penguin Books Ltd.

'Xiahe' by Kathleen Jamie, from *Dream State: The New Scottish Poets*, edited by Donny O'Rourke © 2002. Used by permission of Birlinn Ltd, Edinburgh.

'A Nutshell' by Simon Armitage from *The Universal Home Doctor*, © 2003. Reproduced by permission of Faber and Faber Ltd.

Every effort has been made to trace and contact copyright holders. The publishers would be pleased to hear from any copyright holders not acknowledged here, so that this page may be amended at the earliest opportunity.

Introduction

This book sets out seven aspects of contemporary poetry in an order which will lead, hopefully – if the exercises are followed diligently – to a degree of competence in writing verse. It will also produce a body of work, a first attempt at a cohesive group of poems. This does not guarantee the work will be publishable, but it might give the new writer of poetry a point of perspective from which they can make some informed decisions about each of the matters thus explored.

It is intended to be, straightforwardly, a practical process, focused on learning how to write poetry rather than learning how to read it. Though you are of course welcome simply to read and not to complete the exercises, I would suggest that writing is best approached (and can only be mastered) by doing – not by theorising or reflecting upon what passes here for theory. It is not an intention or a hope that my position on these seven areas should be agreed with. Nor would I claim that these are the seven most obvious or necessary issues a poet need face; or even that outside this book's necessities of progression, these issues would be raised in this order. These are not intended as canonical matters, just as a means of taking the reader as a writer of verse from absolute novice to something more than a beginner.

The chapters are constructed in two halves: there is a discursive section which gives examples and sets exercises; and then there is a dialogue section in which I discuss the issues raised and the assertions made with a prominent poet, so that the reader can examine their veracity, and gain some insight into how seven contemporary poets actually work.

In these dialogues, each poet responds very differently both to the situation of consciously embarking on a dialogue, and to the theme under discussion. Some found it clearer to discuss this through specific poems, others wanted to test it almost as a theory, whilst others simply had very strong opinions they wished to explore. In some cases we arrived at an agreement, in others a compromise, and in a few a discovery. For this reason the dialogues vary in length and in the number of poems cited. I have tended to include those pieces which I felt illustrated a point for the poet, rather than provided an example for me.

The real goal in both halves of the chapters is to establish the ways in which writing poetry may profitably be regarded as a discipline, whilst demystifying its more arcane aspects. To dispel pretention, while encouraging professionalism.

To that end, you should establish your own creative context with which to test the premises set out in this book, regularly buying contemporary poetry and attending readings, involving yourself in your local scene (as far as your temperament will allow – we can't all be extroverts) through writing and reading groups, open mike readings and nearby festivals.

But in general I would suggest that the reader go along with me for the ride, as it were, indulging what are very obviously my obsessions in the order in which I present them, by all means confiding their frustrations, bafflements and disagreements to their personal journal (of which more below). Most importantly, they should do the exercises in the order and the manner suggested, allowing habit its role in establishing creative practice.

Throughout the time you're working with this book, then, you should attempt to write regularly. To that end it may be useful to consider your usual work practice, if you have one, and to make plans if you do not. Do you give yourself a standard time to write, and do you have somewhere at home where you feel relatively secluded? Ask yourself when your creative energies are at their highest, and experiment with writing at different times and in different places. Writers come in all forms, and for each hermit who requires midnight silence in their study, there is a gregarious morning scribbler at the kitchen table. Which do you think you are, and which are you really?

I would also suggest, if you do not already do so, that you begin to keep a creative journal. This is where a writer records the drafts, fragments and ideas for writing that they use to build up finished texts. It can take you through revision after revision, or provide lists of titles, characters, rhymes, descriptions, images and phrases you may or may not use. It can be a diary of responses to the process of composition or to the issues and arguments presented in this book.

It can record your moods, your dreams, your ambitions. It can act as a commonplace book where you store quotes that intrigue or inspire you. It can be filled with photos, drawings, clippings. It can be where you react to books or readings read or attended in parallel to working with this book. Most importantly, it keeps you writing and thinking of yourself as a writer.

You should also carry an easily accessible notebook with you whenever possible, and, if you are not already in the habit of doing so, you should give yourself carte blanche to write in it whatever occurs to you. This can be observations, fleeting thoughts and phrases, things you overheard or thought you overheard. By purchasing this book you are giving yourself permission to write and you should attempt to carry that through into your ordinary behaviour. It doesn't matter if it takes weeks or months to fill that notebook or even to record a single entry: you are still exploring what it means for you to be a writer.

W. N. Herbert

1

Drafting

Part 1

Writing a poem is a process, not a single action. Between the first inkling of a phrase or idea and the published work, there will be a succession of drafts. Each poem begins with a draft; each subsequent draft revises what has gone before. Learning how to revise, how to work through drafts to a publishable poem, is one of the key stages in a writer's development. It could even be said that the act of revision is where the life of a writer is at its richest. Certainly that would be the opinion of Don Paterson:

> It's taken me a pathetically long time to realise that the transcendental joy of poetry isn't getting your book published, reading to an audience of deeply-moved young women, getting your face on the box, winning a prize or anything else – it's the business of composition that blows you away, and the more you can do to savour it, the better.
>
> (Paterson 1996: 159)

What do poets mean by 'the business of composition'? Beginner writers sometimes assume that poetry comes about through a single event called inspiration, which results in a perfect draft. For them 'composition' equates with the first draft. But writing more usually consists of a series of actions, from five finger exercises that get us going (which you'll do shortly), through revisions, to the last correction to a proof. This expanded sense of the 'business' of being a writer is perhaps better termed the practice of writing. In this sense practice is or should be a daily habit, something the initial act of composition very rarely is. Nonetheless, composition can always arise from practice.

It is better to ready ourselves for this to happen, than to wait passively for inspiration. Inspiration is a problematic concept for the student writer, as a focus on its appearance or non-appearance can replace effort or conceal inhibition. Equally, over-attachment to the first draft is an impediment to developing the full richness of any text.

The aligned matters of titling the poem and the consideration of any necessary accompanying text, such as epigraph or footnote, help to frame the process of writing. They are important parts of drafting which we will also explore in this chapter.

Beginning to draft

We are going to begin without discussing our preconceptions about what a poem is, yours or mine. We won't even analyse how we determine what a line of poetry consists of, or whether a poem should rhyme or not. Don't worry, we will engage with all these things in due course, but to begin with we're simply going to start writing.

This is because these matters, important though they are, are essentially arguments, matters of opinion. All truly creative writing begins in the moment we go beyond opinions and arguments, into a territory we may know very little about, and poetry is no different.

This first exercise depends on external stimuli. Later, we'll work with internal stimuli, but it can be good to start with something outside our personal experience, as it focuses our attention on the act of invention, and it doesn't require us to reveal some personal truth (difficult), and to declare it significant (excruciating, if you have a shred of modesty).

The following instructions are quite detailed because I want you to be able to refer back to them in later chapters. Future exercises will assume you are pursuing this method or will clearly request you to depart from it.

When setting a writing exercise I tell people to write for 10–15 minutes without pausing. You can write down whatever you like as long as you keep writing – something you saw a few days ago that might be relevant, a list of possibly related rhymes, an older memory that's suddenly dislodged, an odd image that strikes you, a snippet of dialogue, a description of a person or place, or notes towards all of these. You might find yourself writing in some form of lineation or in a continuous prose block – either is acceptable.

Activity 1.1   Writing

Before you are two images. You can work with one of these, or provide one of your own. One of the things I do whenever I visit libraries, galleries or museums is look at the postcards. If any of them stands out enough to bring my eye back to it repeatedly, or to make me want to take it from a rack and read the back, then I frequently buy it. This is part of the process of building up the reservoir of images and ideas every writer must culti-vate. Taking photographs can work in the same way. When selecting which image to use don't be too deliberate about your motives – the less set your goal in picking a picture, the more unrestrained your writing is likely to be.

Now I would like you to write for 10–15 minutes about the postcard from any of the following premises. (You may find it less distracting to set an alarm, rather than to keep looking at your watch.)

- Imagine what has happened immediately before this image, or what will happen immediately after.
- Focus on an object or person in the image: become that person or object and write in their voice.
- Imagine sending this postcard to someone – it can be anyone living, dead or imaginary – what would you write on the back?
- Imagine receiving this card from someone – living, dead or imaginary – what would they write on the back? Or would they be writing to someone else?

If you find yourself bending the rules – say, instead of becoming a character in the image, you start focusing on their story – go with it. If you start with one premise, then move to another, fine. Remember: you are writing to find something which engages you creatively, not to produce a 'correct' response.

When the period of writing is over (be flexible: if taking another minute means you finish an important sentence, take another minute), then read what you have written. This may seem a trivial point, but it is in fact one of the more significant instructions I can give you. In itself, this action takes us from composition into revision.

Discussion

Most people look at their writing in the sense of glancing over it – they don't read it closely. What they see tends to be as much what they intended to write as what is actually on the page. Phrases and ideas which were never written down hover round the draft, becoming part of their reading experience but no one else's. Simply reading what you've actually written is by no means easy.

Mark those parts which you think might be worth working up later. Indicate those parts you're not sure are working. Write down why in both cases and make suggestions on the page. Ring words that aren't exactly what you want, but could be replaced. Underline rhythms you like the sound of. If your piece was getting interesting when you ran out of time, make a note now on the manuscript of where it might be heading. Don't assume you'll remember (you won't).

This experience of drafting for an exercise is similar to all drafting processes. In each case you are writing to discover: you are looking for a hook, something that engages you enough to keep on writing, to keep on exploring. This can be a draft of a whole poem, just a part of it, or even just a phrase or an image. Each is a valid and profitable result from any exercise.

It's important that you do all this searching on paper. We can have wonderful ideas for things we'd like to write, and it's tempting to day-dream of these instead of getting something down on paper, which will always seem scrappy and inadequate in comparison. But the first suggestion I would make to you is: learn to think on paper.

Write down as much as possible of the process of approaching an idea, and especially the changes you want to make to it when you get a few phrases down. Thinking on paper is the beginning of drafting, and it's always easier to tidy up a messy set of notes than to touch a neat draft.

Go in fear of computers: they produce dangerously 'finished' versions, and they leave few traces of the process. Your previous drafts need to exist if you are to work on them. If you must use computers, save drafts, print out frequently, and get used to marking the page.

Revision

The first draft can be 'given', arriving in a single act of writing, or it can be assembled from a gradual accumulation of elements gathered in our notebooks. You will learn to work with both methods. These are, how-ever, only the beginning of the process of revision. Poems can begin in self-expression, but revision is the means by which that expression is examined in order to arrive at its fullest potential. It is also the route by which we begin to consider and even address an audience. Revision is how a poem matures.

However, revision can also be an obsessive, retarding activity, in which we effectively prevent a poem from reaching its audience as we tinker beyond the point of refinement. It is important to gain a sense of when to stop. Revision can even move in the opposite direction. We may realise that an earlier draft (or a portion of it) is more vital than the current draft. Again, we have to learn through practice, through the act of reading (and listening) to the poem, how best to proceed.

Activity 1.2   Reading

Ironing
I used to iron everything:
my iron flying over sheets and towels
like a sledge chased by wolves over snow,

the flex twisting and crinking
until the sheath frayed, exposing
wires like nerves. I stood like a horse

with a smoking hoof
inviting anyone who dared
to lie on my silver-padded board,

to be pressed to the thinness
of dolls cut from paper.
I'd have commandeered a crane

if I could, got the welders at Jarrow
to heat me an iron the size of a tug
to flatten the house.

Then for years I ironed nothing.
I put the iron in a high cupboard.
I converted to crumpledness.

And now I iron again: shaking
dark spots of water onto wrinkled
silk, nosing into sleeves, round

buttons, breathing the sweet heated smell
hot metal draws from newly-washed
cloth, until my blouse dries

to a shining, creaseless blue,
an airy shape with room to push
my arms, breasts, lungs, heart into.

Read Vicki Feaver on how she produced a draft of 'Ironing' (1994: 10–11) in the following extract from Tony Curtis (1996: 146–50.) Are there any suggestions you can follow in your own drafts?

One way I defeat the critical voices that tell me to give up even before I've started is to keep a notebook. I fill it with shopping lists, student marks, quotations, fragments of a diary, resolutions to lead a more organised life, and, before I commit myself to the terror and potential failure of actually writing a poem, with 'notes' for poems. This is the page headed 'IRONING (notes for)':

Soothing/smoothing/smell/steam
Weight of my hand & arm & shoulder
push into sleeve, the crumpled fabric,
a blouse, silk, purple, violet, crumpled
smooth heat/dampness, the smell of
washed clothes which I know is synthetic
but I am deceived by its smell to believe its natural,
like in a bluebell wood
(Look Back in Anger/Dashing Away with a Smoothing Iron –
I used to sing with my father – he stole my heart away.)
For the years of my children's childhood
I ironed everything (the good mother) even for six months
starch tea-towels (tv ad for spray on starch).
Then for years I ironed nothing.
'Your clothes always look as if they've just come out of the laundry basket,' a woman whose husband fancied me told me.
The iron itself – like a mechanical mouse with a long tail.

[. . .] I don't usually go in consciously for 'Martian-style' similes: But I wanted to make the iron a real physical presence in the poem; to create a series of dream-like and slightly menacing pictures, rather like Paula Rego's nursery-rhyme illustrations. But I rejected the mouse, for its associations with timidity. I replaced it with a whole string of visual similes – a 'sledge chased by wolves over snow', 'wires like nerves' and a 'smoking hoof' – that are not only closer graphically to an iron but that also reflect more effectively the stress and anger of the narrator's emotions. The further images of paper dolls and an 'iron the size of a tug' were added both for their emotional weight and because they came from my life at the time. Like lots of mothers I helped my children cut strings of skirted and trousered figures out of folded paper. Living in Newcastle, I had visited Jarrow to see a ship being launched.

Discussion

Notice how Vicki Feaver's notes for 'Ironing' contain both lines of poetry and lines about the poetry: her notes describe the process of writing and enact it. Notice how her notes are in shortish lines, so that whether a sentence is creative or descriptive, it has the appearance of a line of poetry. The concept of the line is helping her to focus on what the poem may eventually be like. Her notes, in themselves, give her a means of focusing, of meditating on specific words rather than nebulous ideas. This is why you must work on the page.

While you're digesting the process described by Vicki Feaver, I'm going to set you a second exercise. This may seem perverse: you may by now have a few ideas about how you could proceed with your first piece, but I have a simple reason.

Most poets have a number of poems on the go at once, at different stages of completion. This means there is a sense in which they're never blocked: as one piece is being finished, there is always another to polish up. This reduces the pressure the poet feels under to come up with solutions – a better image, a crucial rhyme, a new structure – to the problems of a given poem, until they are ready to turn to it.

It also has a far more important effect: it puts pieces of writing on the back burner. It ensures that the unconscious mind has time to play around with something before you look at it again. This means that when you look at a draft you may find your perspective on it has changed, and – possibly – some of those problems have found their own solutions.

Activity 1.3   Writing

Choose a piece of music lasting about 10 minutes. It is better if the music is unfamiliar, or you haven't played it in a while, so that you don't have a familiar series of associations for it. It can help if the piece is meditative or slow, but it doesn't have to be: experiment with this.

Listen to the music as far as possible without formulating any judge-ments: just allow it to suggest moods or settings, and to create a state of mind. You can make a few notes, but they should not be critical pronouncements on the type of music or performance. Let it produce an emotional or intellectual state – tranquillity or irritation are both acceptable.

Now write for 10–15 minutes from the mood created by the music. You can use it to conjure a physical setting, or recall a memory. Perhaps the different instruments suggested different characters, or a specific event. Perhaps they conjured a garment or a mode of transport. Write as far as possible to concretise what the music suggested.

And when you're done, read your writing and mark on the page how you feel about it and what you intend to do about it.

Activity 1.4   Revision

Now you have two pieces to work from. Pick one and copy the text again onto a new sheet of paper, taking account of all the comments you've made. Take 15–30 minutes, and produce a clean copy which follows your own directions.

Try to follow the phrases according to the physical layout of the first draft, whether you wrote in prose or in some form of lineation. In other words, write, as Vicki Feaver does, as though the piece is already in lines. Some of these may now appear as very long lines with any substituted or extra words you've decided to put in. Think about how you feel about these, even though you may not have originally written with any intention of putting phrases in lines. Do you want to break them into smaller units? Do other such lines now appear too short? If so, mark them, and begin to speculate why. This will prove valuable when we go on to consider why poems might be set out in lines.

Work through those instructions to yourself, and go further: produce that more precise description, include that phrase of dialogue, develop that further incident. Take it as far as you can in the time available, then once more write down on the sheet what you think needs to be done next. This will feed the next draft, and the next.

Discussion

You may find revision takes more time than writing the piece in the first place. Perhaps you're still looking at what is essentially a series of half-ideas, or perhaps you found there was suddenly a new shape appearing.

In either case you're uncovering a basic truth about revision: it is very much like writing the piece all over again. This can have all the mystery and excitement of a new piece of writing, but with this crucial difference: it's within a frame of reference you have already created. You have established some ground rules, and so the speculation, the surprise, is beginning to be directed towards a goal.

That goal, the final or publishable draft, may be a long way away, and there may be many issues of form and audience to consider, but you have begun a dialogue with a specific text. You've begun asking questions of it and allowing it to ask questions of you. In that process you can glimpse the life that other writers pursue for decades. This is the beginning of the same relationship with books – a life's work being shaped in poem after poem – which we intuit when we pick up a volume of collected poems.

At the end of each chapter, try and set aside time for revision. Perhaps in one exercise I'll have given you a choice of which piece of writing to develop – at the end of the chapter develop the others to the same degree. Perhaps something which remains fragmentary may change as the result of thinking about a later chapter. Revision is about finding time to carry these sorts of suggestions through.

Title

The title of a poem is of paramount importance in terms of its impact on the reader. When isolated on the title page of a collection or anthology, it can influence whether the poem is read or not. The space between a title and a first line is charged with anticipation; the moment after the last in which the title is reconsidered is a transformative, reflective zone. And yet it can often be under-considered or even tacked on last: the first thing a reader sees effectively an afterthought. By looking at titles much earlier in the creative process, we will pay them due attention.

There are two main categories of title: the descriptive and the evocative. One appears summative and direct, the other oblique and enticing. Each can in practice have the contrary effect. Each has its uses and subcategories. We will consider which to employ in relation to which poems. Some writers begin with a preponderance of descriptive titles; others may tend to produce more tangential, suggestive titles – if you discover a hitherto unexamined preference for one type, the other can offer new routes for exploration.

Here is a list of titles, some potential, some actual:

What the Cow Thought About the Rain

Otaku (Jap. obsessive)

Source Code

Anthropomorphisation for Beginners

The Shampoo

Between Two Nowheres

The Coral Mother

The Remark

Ghost Words

Things That are Early and Late

The Sea in the Seventeenth Century

Shoes in the Charity Shop

The Nutpacker Suite

The Secret Life of Life

'The Shampoo' would appear to be a descriptive title: this could be a poem about a specific type of shampoo, or an experience of being shampooed. There is an authoritative air about a title like this, a sense almost of definition. Of course the poem may do something very different, in which case there would be a kind of tension created by the type of title itself.

'The Sea in the Seventeenth Century' would also appear to be a descriptive title, but it raises an unresolved question: why the sea at that particular time? Was it noticeably different in that century? Presumably it was less polluted and contained more whales, but why not the sixteenth century, or better still the sea during the Ice Age? So we see that this title is provoking and intriguing us: it is actually a hybrid of the descriptive and the evocative.

'Ghost Words' would appear to be an evocative title, perhaps describing words said by ghosts, or appearing in a ghostly manner, like those at Belshazzar's feast. In fact it's a technical term for words which were printed wrongly in one text, and then taken up in that wrong form by other writers. Technical terms often have this evocative effect, precisely because they are precise terms, but in a specialism we do not recognise. Our response to them perhaps has to be slightly oblique.

'Between Two Nowheres' could be a straightforward evocative title: it suggests a territory that the poem may go on to delineate. It evokes a psychological state, and invites us to read a definition of that state. Of course it could be accurately describing the territory between two towns with the same unusual name.

Activity 1.5   Writing

Select one title from this list that attracts your attention and write for 10 minutes as though you are drafting a piece to be called by this title.

Now read your piece carefully in the usual way, marking any changes on the page. Ask yourself if this is really the title of the draft you have produced? If you were to rename it, thinking of the categories put forward above, what type of title would you give it? Think of two or three appropriate titles in this category and write them down.

Pick one and put it at the head of a new page and, using the principles of revision I've already outlined, write for another 10 minutes, redrafting your piece in order to align it with this new title.

Discussion

Titles give your writing energy. Understanding the different appeal of different kinds of title begins a process of considering our poetry from the point of view of the reader. This perception of the reader becomes increasingly important as you present your work to an audience.

It's good to make lists of possible titles so that you get as used as possible to thinking about the particular energy they can give to a poem. See if you can come up with titles that fall into each of the above categories – or invent further categories. Keep adding to this list as new titles occur.

By the way, the titles already in use are as follows: 'Source Code' (John Burnside), 'The Shampoo' (Elizabeth Bishop), 'Between Two Nowheres' (Norman MacCaig), 'The "Remark" ' (Tom Leonard), 'Things That are Early and Late' (Gillian Allnutt), 'The Sea in the Seventeenth Century' (Paul Farley), 'Shoes in the Charity Shop' (David Constantine). If you've used one of those to produce a draft, you might want to change it.

Epigraphs, glossaries, footnotes

It is a good discipline to write poems which require no exterior information in order to understand and appreciate them. Yet it is not an absolute rule. There are poems which need an obscure term glossed, or an arcane piece of information given as a footnote, and to omit such information would diminish our understanding if not our appreciation. Equally there are poems where the epigraph, that short quote appearing between the title and the first line, establishes a tone or an allusion that the poem then exploits.

Here's what Michael Donaghy says about the appearance of the text upon on the page:

> . . . consider how any printed page of verse or prose, with all its paraphernalia of paragraphs, running heads, marginalia, pagination, footnotes, titles, line breaks and stanzas, can be understood as a diagram of a mental process.
>
> (Donaghy 1999: 11)

Every aspect of the text that appears on a page of poetry has a role to play in its reception, and to overlook elements which have a clear, if secondary, role is short-sighted. We will learn when and how to use these supportive elements and when they are better left off in favour of further revision.

This may seem rather an early point to look at finishing touches like these, but there are two reasons for doing so. As with title, the epigraph, footnote and glosses oblige the writer to consider the reader and what support they might need to understand a poem. This consideration for the reader can't be emphasised soon enough. The second reason is practical: writing from quotes can be a great deal easier than writing from experience. As you'll see in the next two activities, they generate exercises.

Activity 1.6   Reading

Read this list of quotes that follow below. They were harvested from my notebooks over a few months. You too should be copying quotes into your notebooks – if you haven't, begin now. Don't exert too much judgement over why you're copying something in. If it attracts your attention and intrigues you, whether because of what it's saying or how it's saying it, that's good enough for the time being.

And he said, 'So is the kingdom of God, as if a man should cast seed into the ground; and should sleep, and rise night and day, and the seed should spring and grow up, he knoweth not how.'

(Mark 4: 26)

The other half of half-afraid opens many a door.

(Brendan Kennelly)

I have been a thief, a liar, a beggar and a card cheat. I've ridden the Gitanjali Express to Mumbai to run on Chowpatty Beach. I've taken the Coromandel Express to Chennai to swim in the Bay of Bengal. I've sat on top of the Amritsar Mail all the way to the Golden Temple and jumped on the Dehra Dun Express to see the Himalayas, all before I passed ten years old. And I've never once paid for a ticket.

(Homeless boy, Howrah Station, *Guardian*, 16 November 2002)

The word itself is a musical sound.

(Pierre Bernac)

Certain sumo were handicapped by having a quince thrust down their loincloths.

(Source lost (but not invented!))

He loved me more than he did not understand me. He loved me more than he wanted to control me.

(Pedro Almodovar on his father, *Guardian*, 17 August 2002)

Pandas often do handstands when urinating in order to spray their scent high on a tree trunk, say scientists in San Diego.

(*Scottish Sun*, 26 October 2002)

. . . they know exactly what it was like in the old days you'll never be able to see.

(Sam Rowe (age 10) on old people, *Observer*, 1 December 2002)

The silence became strict with absolutely focussed attention, cigarettes were unlit, and drinks stayed on the tables. And in all of the faces, even the most ruined and the most dull, a curious, wary light appeared.

(James Baldwin, *Another Country* (describing the crowd during a sax solo))

Es verdad que lo ignoro todo sobre el
(The truth is I knew nothing about him)

(Borges, 'Isidoro Acevedo')

Epigraphs can operate in three distinct ways in relation to the poem. They can place your new text in relation to a previously written poem by quoting selectively from it, in effect saying, 'my poem is a reaction to this: see if you can work out why.'

They can also provide a crucial piece of information, in which case their role overlaps with that of the footnote, and you must decide: do I want my reader to be aware of this before reading my poem, or shortly afterwards?*

The third use is harder to define: it is when a particular snippet of text, placed between the title and the first line, creates an atmosphere or tone which influences the reader, directing them to look at the poem in a certain way.

Activity 1.7   Writing

Pick a quote that catches your eye. Now go back to your list of titles and select one that might go with it. Now write for 10–15 minutes the piece suggested by the combination of title and quote, using any of the three devices: epigraph, footnote or gloss.

Discussion

Whichever use of epigraph or footnote you tried out, be aware that not all poems will require this kind of accompanying material. Be careful of overburdening a text which can stand up perfectly well by itself.

---

* The footnote is, like the gloss containing an unusual word, slightly after the fact or even outside of the poem, which makes it a good place to store simple facts that are important to understanding the poem, but not a central part of the aesthetic experience.

Sometimes a quote can be an inspiring device to get you into writing a poem, but you don't actually need to include it with the poem when you write it up – it's like the ladder that got you into a locked house, and now you can use the door. Keep collecting quotes, and explore what use you want to put them to. Used sparingly these devices can be highly effective.

Let the act of drafting become second nature to you. Every time you look at a poem, be prepared to scribble something on it, to reconsider the punctuation or the order of the ideas. Check if you can't think of a better title. Establish whether or not anything needs to be footnoted, or whether the footnote or epigraph could be dropped. When you find yourself putting something back in that you've already taken out five times (or vice versa), you'll know that it's time to stop fiddling. Up to that point, however, you're not only producing the best possible version of that poem, you're also training to become the best possible reader of your own work.

References

Curtis, Tony (ed.) (1996) *How Poets Work*. Bridgend: Seren.
Donaghy, Michael (1999) *Wallflowers*. London: The Poetry Society.
Feaver, Vicki (1994) 'Ironing', in *The Handless Maiden*. London: Jonathan Cape Poetry.
Paterson, Don (1996) 'The Dilemma of the Poet', in Tony Curtis (ed.) *How Poets Work*. Bridgend: Seren.

Part 2

Dialogue: Vicki Feaver (VF) and Bill Herbert (BH)

BH: I'd like to start by asking you how you go about drafting a poem. I'm curious, because I've seen your drafts. You set everything out in lines as though the line of the poem and the line of notes about the poem and the line of thoughts – as though they were all equal. Is that the case?

VF: I hadn't really thought of that before but I do begin by making notes. I think that's the most important thing, that I have some raw material. And I think that's right. Because I know poetry is narrow and doesn't fill a whole page, very often I do begin writing it almost like a poem, in quite short lines. So really, I'm like, in some ways, like a painter who uses collage but I make lots of notes, odd bits of notes and then gradually work them up into a poem.

BH: You seem to be describing quite a long process. Is it a long process for you?

VF: Nearly always it is quite a long process, not even just a process that takes place over a day, with lots and lots of drafts, but sometimes a process that can take years. For instance, I've fished out a pile of my old notebooks and I notice that I've got five notebooks in which I've been working on this poem called 'The Handless Maiden'. And the actual poem is about 14 lines, it's a very short poem, but I knew it was a poem I wanted to write because I knew it was a story that was really important to me, and over the years I had various goes at trying to write it and abandoned them.

BH: I think when people start writing, they often feel like the first draft is the most important thing, you know, they've discovered an awful lot through that. And it's perhaps more difficult to learn to settle to living with the drafts, to living with the poem over a long time as you describe. How would you advise people to get on with that process of abiding with the poem?

VF: Well, I think it is very important to keep the drafts and I think the first draft of something is very important and that's why I think it's a really bad idea to have the first draft on a word processor because you can change it so easily, and you are quite apt to do that. Your critical bit of your mind goes in and says, 'Hum, that's not very good, not very smooth, that's not very good,' and you change something that might be quite awkward but actually the poetry might lie in that awkwardness or that strangeness.

BH: To return to this notion of the line and setting out in lines, I think that's important for a couple of reasons. For one thing, it starts the process of thinking of line itself; even if what you are writing is a note, you are still thinking about the limitation of it, there's the shape to it, it's still a unit. The other thing about, as you say, looking around allowing yourself to make notes, is that it seems like a much broader territory. We think about poets honing in and honing in but it seems to me that you start by almost opening out and opening out.

VF: Yes, I think that's really important because I think a good poem is multi-layered. It's hardly ever about just one thing, and if you give the writing process a chance to work in your unconscious – which means writing, sleeping on it, writing, sleeping on it – it can accumulate other layers. And I think in the best poems I've written that's always happened. So, for instance, 'The Handless Maiden' is a story of the handless maiden, but it's also my story as a writer, so I had a chance to think about how it related to me, this feeling of losing your hands and gaining them, which is what happens to the girl in the story. But it also used other things from my life, so, I tried to write the poem before but then I finally did write it when I was staying in a place where there was a river and I could imagine I could be the handless maiden dropping my baby into the water and thinking, yes, there are some trees there, I'd hang her wet clothes up on the trees; there's some moss here, I would dry her with the moss. And those real things went into the poem from the place that I was in. So I think if I'd written the poem, just to begin with, I wouldn't have had a chance for those other things to go into it.

BH: So it's a way of allowing the poem to mature and gain those layers?

VF: Yes. Yes. I think mostly I don't use footnotes to my poems but 'The Handless Maiden' I have given a footnote because there was something about the story that's really interesting. The footnote is: in Grimm's version of this story, the woman's hands grow back because she is good for seven years, but in the Russian version they grow as she plunges her arms into a river to save her drowning baby. The version that I've used is this Russian version, and it was really important to me that her hands grew immediately as a miracle, rather than in the more Christian version that she had to be good for seven years.

The Handless Maiden

When all the water had run from her mouth,
and I'd rubbed her arms and legs,
and chest and belly and back,
with clumps of dried moss;
and I'd put her to sleep in a nest of grass,
and spread her dripping clothes on a bush,
and held her again – her heat passing
into my breast and shoulder,
the breath I couldn't believe in
like a tickling feather on my neck,
I let myself cry. I cried for my hands

my father cut off; for the lumpy, itching scars
of my stumps; for the silver hands –
my husband gave me – that spun and wove
but had no feeling; and for my handless arms
that let my baby drop – unwinding
from the tight swaddling cloth
as I drank from the brimming river.
And I cried for my hands that sprouted
in the red, orange mud – the hands
that write this, grasping
her curled fists.

BH: How important is where you write? We're sitting in a lovely open picture window almost in the Scottish Borders. We're looking out over mountains, there's pheasants, sheep. It's an idyllic setting, but is that sense of place important to how you write?

VF: I suppose as a poet, I'm overwhelmed by big things, like the whole of nature, however beautiful it is, but I think I fix on small things that usually have some metaphorical significance for me, more than the thing itself. So for me, for instance, a gun is an object – I didn't even know I was going to write a poem about a gun. I've just been looking through my old notebooks and I found the first mention of this poem, of the gun: I put, 'The gun fills me with foreboding. It is an air rifle. To get a shotgun you have to get a licence. It costs £300.' I mean, very dull, boring things. And then I move on from that to sort of thinking what does the gun look like and I haven't really looked at it yet, I'm too afraid to. It's like something out of the Wild West. It's huge and sinister. It fills the whole kitchen table. It's made of dark wood and black metal. There's a case of pellets, they look like curled up metal, I can't even read what I've written, but the point is that then in the poem I've got something about the gun, laying it on the kitchen table, stretched out like something dead itself. So, in a way I'm then gradually moving towards that poetry, but I'm just beginning with very prosaic things.

BH: A lot of people, I think, believe that they must go to an inspiring place to be inspired. The idea that this landscape is too big and that you need the particular, the specific, and then from that you embark on setting out an inner landscape, and there's a definite journey there – I think that's tremendously helpful.

VF: But then small things from my environment come in because at the end of that poem there's 'the king of death stalking out of the winter woods, his black mouth sprouting golden crocuses'. And when I look in my diary, when I wrote that poem, these woods here were full of yellow crocuses.

BH: What part does the paraphernalia of the poem play – the title, the footnote and all these other things? Is that part of the actual drafting, the genesis of the poem or is it something that happens later?

VF: I have very short titles generally. They are very short and to the point: 'The Handless Maiden', it's just the title of the story. So, my titles are very simple really, they relate to the thing – I mean, 'The Gun' is a very simple title. [Laughter]

BH: You seem to be describing them as descriptive titles, but then I remember being struck by 'Bitch Swimming', which is a descriptive title, but it's enormously evocative and contrary as a phrase. It covers a great deal of territory, very briefly.

VF: In my new book, I've got two titles which I really love. One is 'The Man Who Ate Stones', which I think immediately throws up a sort of mystery, and next to it is a poem called 'The Woman Who Talked To Her Teeth'. [Laughter]

BH: 'The Man Who Ate Stones' is an extraordinary title. Where did that come from?

VF: Well, it's really strange, because my husband is a psychiatrist and I thought he would tell me wonderful stories about patients, and he refuses to tell me anything. But, just once, I was at the hospital where he works, and one of the therapists talked about a patient who ate stones, and I thought this was amazing, but I still didn't get any details, and so I just began to think why would somebody eat stones? Once, years ago when I was a student, I took cannabis and I felt I was going to go through the ceiling of the house, so that's one of the images that comes into it, taking this cannabis and just thinking I would float off and saying please hold me down. [Laughter]

The Man Who Ate Stones
He had never felt so light:
his skin like the paper of kites,

his bones like the inside of Maltesers.
He thought he was going to float

through the roof of the house,
drifting through space

like an astronaut
untethered from his craft.

He begged his wife to hold him down
but she just laughed.

He drove to the beach, and knelt
at the edge of the sea,

swallowing pebbles to weight
his stomach with ballast.

The water was black, except where the moon
lit fires in the breaking waves.

He saw the god whose home
is under the ocean's storms –

the bubbles of his breath,
shooting to the surface.

Here was another man
who had to eat stones.

He plunged into the burning water
to meet him.

BH: I know that you don't write in conventional forms. Is there a sense of discovering the form of the poem, is that part of the drafting? Do you see the shape of the poem before or do you discover it through the drafting?

VF: I think it's always a case of discovering it. There's something I like that Ezra Pound said, when you use a form, like a sonnet, it's like a pot that you have to fill; so it exists already and you have to pour the words in. And then he talks about free verse as being like organic form, like a tree that grows itself, and I think that's how I see the form of my poems, and quite often the form doesn't come until quite late on.

BH: The thing I was curious about was whether the poems shared their lives with each other, not necessarily in a sequential manner, but when you get to the end of that 10 years, when you produce that book, whether it was something that grew with you, or whether it's something that comes about as a result of these separate processes and somehow they come together and they make a new thing.

VF: I think it must be both because I'm struck by one thing and I write that poem and all my attention is directed. I don't work on several poems together. I work on one poem and my attention is directed towards getting that poem right in some way. And sometimes I abandon them and sometimes I come back to them, but I just focus on one at a time. But then I discover, when I've written, well, the book I've just finished, which is an accumulation of poems written over 10 years – it's called *The Book Of Blood* – it was strange, when I was beginning to put a book together, I just realised how many poems connected with that theme.

BH: Did you allow this to grow? It wasn't like you said, well I must cover this aspect, this aspect, this aspect and you had a master plan; it was something which came through the process of writing?

VF: Yes. Yes, I haven't thought, oh I'll write that poem because it belongs to that. It's quite strange – the gun poem, I hadn't, at that point, decided to call the book *The Book Of Blood*, although obviously that so well fits in with that theme. And there's another poem, 'The Sacrifice', which came from a drawing that I saw in the Art Gallery in Edinburgh of some girls leading a bull to sacrifice and, of course, that also fits in with the theme, and I suppose it must be because my mind was revolving round those areas that I was interested in that drawing, but I didn't realise that. Quite often your mind does these things of its own accord and it's only afterwards that you see the logical connections.

The Gun
Bringing a gun into a house
changes it.

You lay it on the kitchen table,
stretched out like something dead

itself: the grainy polished wood stock
jutting over the edge,
the long metal barrel
casting a grey shadow
on the green-checked cloth.

At first it's just practice:
perforating tins
dangling on orange string
from trees in the garden.
Then a rabbit shot
clean through the head.

Soon the fridge fills with creatures
that have run and flown.
Your hands reek of gun oil
and entrails. You trample
fur and feathers. There's a spring
in your step; your eyes gleam
like when sex was fresh.

A gun brings a house alive.

I join in the cooking: jointing
and slicing, stirring and tasting –
excited as if the King of Death
had arrived to feast, stalking
out of winter woods,
his black mouth
sprouting golden crocuses.

VF: I think the poem began with, 'At first it was just practice, aiming at tins, dangling on orange strings from trees in the garden', so it didn't begin with 'Bringing a gun into a house changes it'. It was just completely different really, because I've got things here, 'I stand in the steam from a pot of wood-pigeon and see the kitchen's *nature morte* begin to live, dancing spoons and spatulas, glinting pans.' So I had this idea of the kitchen coming alive in the steam which I rejected from the poem because it was about the gun, and in the last stanza, which reads now, 'I join in the cooking, jointing and slicing, stirring and tasting,' which is very much to do with just these activities – it's all verbs – and, what I at one stage had was, 'I join in the cooking, marinade rabbits in wine and garlic, braise woodpigeon with brandy and fennel.' And I think why I changed that, thinking about it, that it's too much like, here's the goddess of cooking, it's too much like a cook. [Laughter] It was too much like Nigella writing a cookery book. The image, 'excited as if the King of Death had arrived to feast,' I think was to come into the poem really quite late on. I haven't got all the drafts here but quite early on I'd got everything dances, spoons and spatulas, shiny pans, a yellow colander, a gun mouth sprouting golden crocuses. And the idea of the King of Death coming to feast, I'm just trying to think where that comes from. I can't think but it must be this: I think I might have been trying to write a poem about Persephone at the same time, and that got into it, because Persephone, who's the goddess of spring who comes with all these crocuses, is married to the King of Death in his underworld in the winter. And I've got these winter woods in the poem and I think that's when I wrote it.

BH: One of the things your poems do is almost effortlessly step into the mythic and step out of it again. To me it's got this medieval context, I see the great striding skeleton, from the frescos in Pisa, after the plague. It's a very powerful moment, but it's kind of an eruption, isn't it? Something enters the poem at that point and I suppose the key thing is that you waited for him to arrive, you kept the draft going until he got there.

VF: I think that's right because he connects both with the gun and the killing, but he also connects with Persephone and her sort of darkness, but then her bursting out into spring with all these flowers which were in my garden at the time, all these crocuses.

BH: Your work, you talk about it operating on a number of levels, sometimes some of those levels are really strong, primal, disturbing. How do you live with that when you are working? Is it upsetting? How do you integrate it with your normal life?

VF: I think in some ways it's therapeutic really to use poetry as a way of connecting with the shadow parts of yourself, and I think too that poetry as art becomes distanced from the ordinary, the poet who is this normal human person who is living. So I think the two things are separate. I think, maybe, when you first begin to write poetry and you just write very raw poems about your emotions, then in a way that can be very disturbing. But once you begin thinking of poetry as an art form, that you are drawing in all these other things and that you are working on the language of it – because this poem didn't just come out like that, it's also a poem that's got draft after draft after draft in my notebook – that in a way it becomes almost detached from yourself.

BH: Most poets are slow and most people who start writing are similarly slow because they are unsure what to pick or how to find that first impetus. So, have you any advice on how to be a slow poet?

VF: Yes, I think it's really important to read other people's poems. I know that for me when I've had periods of not writing, just reading the poems that I enjoy or reading a good anthology . . . I think, when I first began writing, I didn't really know about contemporary poetry at all. I read Blake and Wordsworth and I loved their poems. I didn't really read women poets, I didn't know about Stevie Smith and Adrienne Rich and Sylvia Plath and I found poetry a terrifying thing. It's reading contemporary poems and poems in a contemporary voice . . . you might think reading other people's poems would make you just copy their voices, so that you wouldn't be original, but I don't think that's true. I think, actually, you find a voice to answer back and it's like a sort of dialogue with other poets. But you only discover it in each poem you write, so it's like growing your hands again, you have to keep rediscovering it. And you just have to do it, you just have to let go of all your terrors and fears about words and language and poetry and the fact that it's so difficult, because, actually it isn't difficult to fling a few words down. I think, in a way, you have to be like one of those action painters who hurls the paint at the canvas and you can always tidy things up afterwards, you can do anything. But if you've got any scaredness at all, just go for it, just, just fling the words into the air, you know, write at white hot speed, get them on to the paper and then think about and then read them through, okay, in a sort of cold way and a critical way, but don't let the inhibitions get in the way of that sort of initial impulse. In a way, I ought to be giving that advice to myself because I can spend ages thinking 'Oh I can't write. It's too difficult. I've got nothing to say any more.' But there's always something to say. I think some of the most wonderful poems are written about the simplest

29

things. I just think that the subject isn't a problem; it's actually finding a way of addressing it that engages with everything that you care about, with other things in your life. I think for me, because I really love painting, visual images are really, really important. They are important to me, but actually those are really good things for a poet to be interested in because they make poems vivid. So I'm probably more interested in the look of things than the sound of things, but somebody else might be more interested in the sound of things and get those into their poems, or they might be a very touchy-feely person and they'd get those things, the feel of something into their poem. Or they might be some person who's really good at listening to dialogue, and being good at listening to dialogue makes good poems, someone like Robert Frost has got loads of dialogue in his poems. It's just being alert to details really but then being able to connect those to much more profound things, but not in the grand Victorian way, laying your emotions in too extreme a way, just dealing with those things through quite ordinary things – a piece of cheese, a piano, anything really, it doesn't matter.

References

Feaver, Vicki (1994) 'The Handless Maiden', in *The Handless Maiden*. London: Jonathan Cape, p. 12.

Feaver, Vicki (2003) 'The Man Who Ate Stones', in *Girl in Red and Other Poems*. Edinburgh: Scottish Book Trust, p. 20.

Feaver, Vicki (2003) 'The Gun', in *Girl in Red and Other Poems*. Edinburgh: Scottish Book Trust, p. 22.

2

Line

The line is the basic device which distinguishes poetry from prose. It does this by focusing on a different unit from the grammatical phrase. Whether a line forms a complete sentence or an incomplete one, whether it forms a musical phrase or strikes a harsh note, its purpose is clearly not limited to revealing sense. It is a unit of attention. The line momentarily removes a selection of words from the normal flow of language and suspends it for examination.

You might compare this to the instant of consciousness – approximately three seconds long – which neuroscientists believe constitutes the present moment. In that brief space we can appreciate the language contained in the line on a number of levels: its rhythm, its sound, its ideas, its phrase-making or its metaphoric content. We can even relate it to previous lines and anticipate its relationship with subsequent ones.

At this stage we will consider the line firstly as a free verse unit, and then as a syllabic form. We will also look at the roles played by stress and alliteration in forming the line. More formal analysis of metre will be covered in Chapter 6.

The line break

Where we choose to break a phrase in order to begin a new line has consequences for the entire poem. If we break it at the end of a clause or sentence, then we reinforce grammatical sense with an unspoken emphasis. If we break within a phrase, then we introduce a sense of incompletion which can pull us forward through the poem, almost demanding that we make sense of the line by reading on. Conversely, if we break within a phrase and follow that with a space, whether an indentation or a stanza break, then we create a note of suspension, implying that the normal progression of a sentence can contain spaces where the reader can pause.

Activity 2.1   Reading

Let's look at what this might mean in relation to a poem, Liz Lochhead's 'Dreaming Frankenstein' (1984: 11). Before I discuss this poem, I should just make a comment about the poetry I will be presenting in this book. Each poem is there to illustrate a technical point. While it can be fascinating to explore the meanings of each piece, your primary focus must be on the issue under discussion. Don't feel you have to fully understand every nuance of a poem before you can proceed.

The technical point with this piece is its line breaks: can you find reasons for each line break Liz Lochhead makes?

> **Dreaming Frankenstein**
> for Lys Hansen, Jacki Parry and June Redfern
>
> She said she
> woke up with him in
> her head, in her bed.
> Her mother-tongue clung to her mouth's roof
> in terror, dumbing her, and he came with a name
> that was none of her making.
>
> No maidservant ever
> in her narrow attic, combing
> out her hair in the midnight mirror

on Hallowe'en (having eaten
that egg with its yolk hollowed out
then filled with salt)
– oh never one had such success as this
she had not courted.
The amazed flesh of her
neck and shoulders nettled
at his apparition.

Later, stark staring awake to everything
(the room, the dark parquet, the white high Alps beyond)
all normal in the moonlight
and him gone, save a ton-weight sensation,
the marks fading visibly where
his buttons had bit into her and
the rough serge of his suiting had chafed her sex,
she knew – oh that was not how –
but he'd entered her utterly.

This was the penetration
of seven swallowed apple pips.
Or else he'd slipped like a silver dagger
between her ribs and healed her up secretly
again. Anyway
he was inside her
and getting him out again
would be agony fit to quarter her,
unstitching everything.

Eyes on those high peaks
in the reasonable sun of the morning,
she dressed in damped muslin
and sat down to quill and ink
and icy paper.

Discussion

That first line break alerts us to an unusual mind: 'She said she'. Many people would want to keep the verb with the subject by running those first

two lines together. But then they would have that funny line ending 'in' – in what? Ah yes, her head. And then we have the parallel phrase 'in her bed'. It might seem sensible to write these lines as:

> She said she woke up with him
> in her head, in her bed.

But think how reasonable that makes the phrasing sound. This is a nightmarish event, and Lochhead's lineation follows that by cutting into our expectations. These are instances of broken phrases pulling us onward, into the poem.

Later in the poem, we find the more normal usage of breaking the line where the phrases naturally pause, using emphasis and strong nouns, but notice how these line endings are suited to the more sober note the poem is striking at this point:

> Later, stark staring awake to everything
> (the room, the dark parquet, the white high Alps beyond)
> all normal in the moonlight . . .

In fact the poem alternates between breaking the phrase up, and ending neatly on it (as the whole poem ends), in order to reflect its subject matter. That subject – the violence of an inspiration which changed Mary Shelley's life, and entered popular iconography in the shape of *Frankenstein* – is caught up with the gender of the speaker, and, like the Vicki Feaver poem, contemplates how hard it can be for women to find a voice. This means, when we glance back at the first line, that what sounded fragmentary on first reading can now be said to hold an assertion: 'She said she' – she found a way of expressing herself.

The way the line can interrupt the run of sense to isolate and fleetingly suggest another meaning is one of the things only poetry can do. And it does this through exploitation of the line break.

It may seem a basic statement to make about the line that it must contain something, but this actually does a great deal of the hard work without going on to discuss metre. If we stick for now with just the idea of the line containing something, then perhaps we can see why many poets are keen on form.

Imagine a mother holding her child, then imagine a stranger holding the same child. One gesture has been built up from experience, it is caring and practical; the second is more spontaneous – it is equally careful, but less tutored, there is a threat that the child may be dropped, and slightly less emotional investment in it if it is. Imagine a fisherman holding a fish: his relation to the fish is much crueller, but it is also full of pride. It too is careful, but that is because it is the nature of the fish to be difficult to hold.

Each of these scenarios could describe the attitude of the poet towards a line of verse – the sure, loving crafter; the excited but uncertain beginner; the pure, almost cold technician. Each of them could describe the way that a poetic line holds words: the end-stopped, memorable unit; the tentative, could-be-different solution; the fluid, onward-driving, incomplete phrase.

Activity 2.2   Writing

Take one of the pieces you have been working on and spend 10–15 minutes breaking it into lines. By all means think about Lochhead's line breaks, and hold onto the idea that each line must contain something – but be prepared to break your lines on impulse and break them on feel. You will build up by this means a sense of what a line can be for you that will hold true whether you're writing in free verse or metrical poetry.

You should revise this draft after reading the next paragraph (or apply the same principles to one of your other drafts).

What is a line holding if not metrical beats? It could hold an image; an unusual word or phrase; a tone; a rhythm, whether analysed or not. It could hold a bit of alliteration; it could hold all you can say in a single breath; it could have a rhyme at the end of it you want the reader to notice. Lines in poems, whether free verse or metrically precise, will contain one or more of these. When you try justifying to yourself why one unit is a line, and why another isn't quite, ask yourself: 'What is it holding?' Is it holding enough to justify the reader looking on this for the whole three seconds of their present moment?

Syllabics

One of the consequences of limiting the length of a line is that we introduce a concept of duration. By weighing up how long a line should be relative to the other lines in a poem we begin calculating its actual length, and one of the simplest ways of doing this is to count the number of syllables it contains. The word 'sy-lla-bics' contains three syllables. The line 'all-nor-mal-in-the-moon-light' contains seven.

If we declared that all the lines in a poem should be seven syllables long, this would impose a shape, albeit one that took no account of the rhythm of a line. But it would offer a limit for the flow of the sentence to either meet or run over, and this gives us an important principle to work with. These two antagonistic principles – the flow of the sentence and the limit of the line – provide one of the bases of all form. From the tension between them arises the unique marriage of form and content that makes up a poem.

Activity 2.3   Writing

This exercise is in two parts, one consisting of free writing in the manner you're accustomed to, and the other a slower piece of shaping.

I'd like you to write on the following theme: an animal you identify with. It can be a real animal you have owned, a family pet, perhaps; or a real animal you have seen in the wild or in a zoo or even on television. It can be an animal you've never seen, but have read about or seen pictures of; even an imaginary or mythic animal. The important thing is that you feel the animal embodies you in some way in its characteristics or behaviour – in the case of a pet, it could sum up a period of your life. Give yourself 10–15 minutes.

Afterwards, make your usual notes.

The second part of the exercise can be done immediately or later, depending on the time and energy you have available.

I'd like you to select one number from seven to eleven, and another from three to five. The first number is your syllable count, the number of syllables permitted per line of your redraft. The second is the number of lines per stanza, or verse paragraph. Yes, I know we're supposed to do stanzas later, but I want you to start wondering about these units within a poem – firstly so that some groundwork is done; and secondly because it gives you two things to work on within this draft. Trying to do more than one thing at a time in creative terms helps bring your unconscious into the process.

Now, take 10–15 minutes to rewrite your first draft, ensuring that each line fits your chosen syllable count, and that the poem is formed into regular stanza units.

Discussion

One of the effects such an exercise is likely to induce is enjambment, or the running over of meaning from one line to another, and even from one stanza to another. You might even find yourself breaking some poly-syllabic words in two to fit in with this artificially imposed shape. In all this there is a sense of transgression, that the containers, whether of the line, the stanza or even the word, have all been broken. Good. The issue about lineation which this exercise brings out is: purpose.

As we saw in the Lochhead poem, there is nothing inherently wrong with lines running on in this fashion, it's more a matter of determining why it's happening, and whether this furthers the sense of the poem – its intention, its drive, its rhythm – or runs counter to it.

This exercise underscores what has already been said about line: it is there to alert the reader to a sense of intent. It reinforces the meaning, the pace and the rhythm of what is being said. Depending on how the sense fits into the line, it can even help a statement become memorable. Syllabics run slightly counter to our instincts about line because they can feel arbitrary.

Of course a piece could be rewritten so that the phrases fall more exactly within the syllabic frame – and that frame can be altered to allow them to do so. But this doesn't address an underlying issue which the use of syllabics has to overlook. Syllabics just count, they can't measure, so to limit ourselves to them is to be insensitive to one of the dominant effects in poetry, the rhythm. Our language is stress-based, which means that every line contains a number of lighter or heavier stresses or beats. How light, how heavy, is an act of measurement, and this leads us on to the rudiments of metre.

Alliteration and other patterns

The oldest way of constructing a line in English poetry is by introducing alliteration, finding two or more words that begin with the same sound. The same principle is used in tabloid headlines to catch the reader's eye and ear. A regular pattern of alliteration causes us to count, to measure the line in some manner, and this imposes a shape, if not shapeliness.

Further, because English is a stress-based language, having a certain number of alliterative words will necessarily introduce a certain number of stresses. Consider the line 'Then the would-be assassin attacked me with an anglepoise.' There are several non-alliterating words in this sentence, some of which contain stresses, and so counting the alliterative terms only gives us a minimum number. But it is arguable, nonetheless, that alliteration helps to introduce a sense of rhythm.

In traditional alliterative verse the stress in the alliterating word is often focused on its opening syllable. This is to help the listener hear what's happening. The word 'anglepoise', being stressed '**ang**lepoise', emphasises the first syllable and therefore obviously alliterates on 'a'. The word 'at**tacked**', though it also begins with 'a', emphasises the second syllable, and so is less noticeably alliterating – the 't' of 'tacked', thanks to the stress, dominates. (How would you assess 'assassin'?) From counting alliterative words to noticing stresses in this way involves a small refinement of the ear, but it has enormous consequences.

If you can detect stresses then you can count them, and thus begin to think of lines as possessing beats. If you can regularise the number of strong beats in a line, then with or without alliteration, you have the metrical competence to write what is known as accentual verse, verse which is aware of the main accents or stresses which are distributed through English. Accentual verse is a category which includes both the medieval ballad and contemporary rap.

Activity 2.4   Reading

Read this section from the 'Age of Anxiety' by W.H. Auden, from *Collected Longer Poems* (1988 [1968]: 337). Identify the points at which Auden is alliterating.

> If you blush, I'll build breakwaters.
> When you're tired, I'll tidy your table.
> If you cry, I'll climb crags.
> When you're sick, I'll sit at your side.
> If you frown, I'll fence fields.
> When you're ashamed, I'll shine your shoes.
> If you laugh, I'll liberate lands.

When you're depressed, I'll play you the piano.
If you sigh, I'll sack cities.
When you're unlucky, I'll launder your linen.
If you sing, I'll save souls.
When you're hurt, I'll hold your hand.
If you smile, I'll smelt silver.
When you're afraid, I'll fetch you food.
If you talk, I'll track down trolls.
When you're on edge, I'll empty your ash-tray.
If you whisper, I'll wage wars.
When you're cross, I'll clean your coat.
If you whistle, I'll water wastes.
When you're bored, I'll bathe your brows.

Discussion

This is a deft piece of craftsmanship by a technical master: not only are there three examples of alliteration per line, but there is a clear repeated structure, an imposed shape of couplets beginning 'If' and 'When'. You can see this is as constructed a thing as, say, a poem rhyming in couplets.

Notice what he does in the line 'When you're ashamed, I'll shine your shoes' – 'ashamed' would appear to alliterate on 'a', but because the part of the word we stress most when we say it is actually the 'sh' sound, he can alliterate on that. Note also the licence he allows himself in 'When you're on edge, I'll empty your ash-tray' – two alliterations on 'e', then a word beginning with 'a'. Well, it is a vowel, and I suppose it sounds closer to 'e' than 'o' or 'u' would. But it just goes to show: don't box yourself into a corner if it means the poem can't proceed. Poetic rules are flexible, and sometimes the sign of a master is how he or she bends them!

Auden harks back in this poem to a use of alliteration which persisted in English poetry into the fourteenth century. Its last major practitioner was William Langland, the author of *Piers Plowman*. Pat Boran makes an interesting point about alliteration in relation to this poet:

> . . . Langland was writing for listening audiences. He was 100% interested in sound. You might say that the invention of printing

relieved poets of some of that responsibility (or deprived them of some of those riches, depending on your point of view), but certainly once books began to appear, the whole shape and organisation of English poetry changed . . . Chaucer was one of the first English poets to recognise 'the emerging literate mindset of his courtly audience', and his more complex sound and sentence structures confirm this. He wrote in the knowledge that if something was missed it could be returned to, re-read. It is believed Chaucer died the year Gutenberg was born. The invention of movable type revolutionised writing and printing, and therefore poemmaking too, as has, to an extent, every major communications invention since.

(Boran 1999: 80–1)

Chaucer, of course, rhymed. Arguably alliteration has an air of being an antiquated, almost crude device: poets use it, but it is not the dominant structural principle, more an occasional musical reinforcement. Nonetheless alliteration points us to the way poetry is older than most fiction – a form very happily married to the printing press. Poetry's reliance on music as an attention-grabber and an aide-memoire has survived into the computer age, and alliteration is still a primary building block in that musicality.

Activity 2.5   Writing

Write an alliterative love poem, but not to a human being. It can be domestic: to your favourite food, your favourite household appliance, or your car. It can be decidedly non-domestic, aspirational or even fantastical: to your favourite local monument, fictional character or planet.

What it must be is alliterative: I would go for two clear alliterative sounds in each line – three if you dare, or on an occasional basis. Try to keep the space between these sounds short enough for the relation between them to be audible. This doesn't mean writing in short lines: experiment with length and placement.

Discussion

Depending on how concise your lines are, you can assume they will contain a minimum of three beats: one for each alliterating word, and probably at least one for the part of the sentence which separates them. Let's look again at two lines from Auden's poem:

> When you're on edge, I'll empty your ash-tray.
> If you whisper, I'll wage wars.

If we read this out loud, listening for emphasis, we can certainly say that, in the first line, we would stress the first syllable of each of the alliterating words: '**edge**', '**emp**ty', '**ash**-tray'. That's how we pronounce those words in ordinary conversation, and Auden has placed them in the line so that they form a little rhythm. This rhythm alerts us to another word he's stressing: '**When**'. So this line has four sounds in it we say with a little more emphasis than the others.

But when we say the second line aloud, we can say that, although it has three words beginning with 'w', the rhythm doesn't place equal emphasis on all three of them. '**Whisp**er' and '**wars**' seem to have a certain weight, but you have to emphasise '**I'll**' a little more than 'wage', both to make sense of the line, and to catch its rhythm. Of course, if we follow the pattern of the first line, and put some emphasis on '**if**' as we did on '**when**', then a pattern becomes clear:

> **When** you're on **edge**, I'll **emp**ty your **ash**-tray.
> **If** you **whi**sper, **I'll** wage **wars**.

If we count syllables, we can see that the first line has one or two syllables between the stressed sounds; and the second has one. So the first line feels more expansive, and the second tighter.

So hearing beats has two components: finding where the main stresses are in a word in ordinary conversation, and finding how many more lightly stressed or unstressed syllables lie between them. In order to get a rhythm going, there has to be a fairly regular occurrence of beats with not too many of the less stressed or unstressed syllables in between.

If there is a regular number of beats in every line, then a certain pattern has been achieved, and you are, effectively, writing accentual verse. Later on, we'll discuss what happens when these beats combine with regular patterns of unstressed syllables. But for now, the important element is to begin listening and counting.

Activity 2.6   Revision

Look at your alliterative piece from the previous activity again. Check whether your alliterative words all have the main stress on the alliterating part of the word, and see if you can find the other words in each phrase which have a roughly equal stress. How many syllables apart are they, and how many syllables are there in each of your lines? Can you rephrase them to make the rhythm more audible?

The principle of containment alerts us to the line as a unit of attention. It enables us to present our phrases to a reader in such a way as to allow them to dwell on them momentarily and to notice and appreciate the particular linguistic effect that is going on. As writers, it enables us to begin to measure what we are saying rhythmically, to create pattern, and to build up music. It is not the case that none of these things would be going on if we were writing in prose, but it is certainly true that the line is a helpful unit when it comes to shaping what we have to say.

From this chapter on, experiment with writing your exercises in lines, reserving the right to sketch things out in prose if need be, but always revising towards a notion of the line.

References

Auden, W.H. (1988 [1968]) 'Age of Anxiety', in *Collected Longer Poems*. London: Faber and Faber.

Boran, Pat (1999) *The Portable Creative Writing Workshop*. Cliffs of Moher, Co. Clare: Salmon.

Lochhead, Liz (1984) 'Dreaming Frankenstein', in *Dreaming Frankenstein & Collected Poems*. Edinburgh: Polygon.

Part 2

Dialogue: Gillian Allnutt (GA) and Bill Herbert (BH)

BH: When people approach poetry first of all, one of the things which confronts them is the fact it's in lines. And they almost think why is this prose norm – which they are coming from sometimes – why is it being broken up? It would be nice to get your take on just what are lines for.

GA: Certainly, when I work in primary schools, I often ask, 'What's the difference between a story and a poem?' And I'm after the answer, 'Poems come in short lines, one underneath the other.' I guess it gives you space to think between one line's end and the beginning of the next; spaces in which to imagine, spaces in which to make pictures.

BH: How do you go about deciding where the space should be? Is there a natural instinct that people can develop, or is there something that you are aware of very specifically doing in order to create that space?

GA: I've changed my own writing practice because of teaching adults in workshops and wanting them to write in the workshop time, and wanting to write myself and then read out what I've written, as well as them, so that I lay myself on the line and create an atmosphere of trust. And I find, if I start trying to write a poem in a workshop in 20, 30, 40 minutes, I can't often come up with something that's read-outable and so I've evolved the practice of writing prose in workshops, with a poem in the back of my mind, and when I get home I sit down at the computer and I type my prose piece out one sentence per line and then I take it from there.

BH: That's actually quite a good starting premise for someone who's maybe coming to poetry from prose: to start with that idea of the sentence per line. Can you talk us through a specific example where you are doing this, this one sentence per line?

GA: (reads)

The Silk Light of Advent
Mara sighs over the silks laid out on the rosewood windowsill.
She would rather look into the fire.
It is terribly hard to decide when the garden is dead.
In December the lake is dumb.
There are no leaves left and no wind left to stir them.
Later in life she will say that the light on the Somme was like that then.
Mara sighs over the skeins.
She is neither girl nor woman.
Her brother is in uniform.
There is no one left to walk with in the morning.
Her mother has always left her alone.
The newspaper's forbidden.

The angel will be embroidered, soon, by evensong.
After that there'll be no more sewing.
In the beginning needles were made of bone.
The angel will come in the afternoon.
Later in life she will know the value of precision.
At two o'clock in the afternoon she will say again and again.
Her brother will not be missing then.
He writes he is learning to smoke and polish buttons.
She will get up from the fire.
She'll walk slowly back to the windowsill.
She'll know then that the angel's hands are dumb.
The eyes are gone.
There are sockets of silk she will never embroider for him.
The lake is dry, like bone.
The angel is terribly beautiful.
She won't be able to cry.

BH: The interesting thing about hearing you read that, Gillian, is that the space between the sentences seems constant but the sentences themselves are of such varying lengths that it's almost as though you're putting silences in, but in very different places, so it creates a very individual, a very particular rhythm.

GA: I think, one of the things, this is a very depressing poem. It's about her being aware that her brother has been killed, at the moment at which he's been killed. And, I think, most of the lines, a lot of the lines end with 'um, un, ul' and I have the feeling as if I'm pushing the audience down into the ground. But also the poem is like a collage and, I think, one of the reasons I want one sentence per line is that I want to keep it simple because I'm doing something that, to my mind, is quite complicated with time. I'm dealing with her present and her future at the same time and there's a bit from the present, a bit from the future and another bit from the present and it darts about and it is complicated and that is partly also why I leave gaps, I think, to give people time to take in the rather complicated thing that's happening.

BH: There's something there about the line having a use, having a purpose, because what you were saying about the different past, present and future, different tenses of her life, is reflected in the way that the sentences are longer and shorter. There is a sense of the sentence darting about before meeting, again, this kind of inevitable silence, the space of realisation for the character, but also for the reader.

GA: Yes, I think that's a good point. I like the idea of the sentence darting about. It starts and it, no, that's no good, it starts here and, oh no, it goes back there. Perhaps to reflect the traumatic nature of the experience and ending up, as you say, with silence.

BH: I think it's very interesting that you are prepared to change your practice as a writer in order to meet your practice as a teacher and in a case like this we can see where it fits in to your work. I often feel that some students regard their teachers as doing something almost separate from what they are doing.

GA: Yes, like I said it's important to me to lay myself on the line, to remind myself of how difficult it can be to read out what you have just written. I mean, I've done years and years of poetry readings but, sometimes, if I embark on reading out what I've just written in a workshop I can be quite shaky because it's very close to the bone and I suppose I haven't got my professional jacket on.

BH: I like that phrase, 'Lay yourself on the line!' I'm wondering if it might be good to look at a poem where you extend beyond the line or you break into it in a different way and proceed by example through that notion of line break.

GA: (reads)

Child

She is heavier than air, a little heavier.

I shall carry her on my shoulder.

How did I come by her? Did I beget her?

Can I, how can I, abandon her to her stony desolation?

I shall walk with her as if I wore the whole Sahara on my
    shoulder –
wind, sand, sun and all of it frail as an aeroplane –
shadow and whole.

She has come to me.

'She is frail now, frail,' my mother said of her mother,
my grandmother in the cottage hospital.

'The light shows through her, she is full
of holes

and, when I lift her, lighter, almost,
than air.'

BH: Now in that poem I think we could hear the voice stopping, hesitat-
ing, moving on. To what extent is the line break measuring that, or
capturing that motion?

GA: To quite a large extent I think. The first four lines, in fact, have
double spaces between them so they are actually stanzas, separate
one line stanzas, and they're myself considering this strange child.
She's not very heavy, oh I'll carry her on my shoulder but where did
she come from? And I can't just abandon her, can I? And then
there's a sense of there's a decision, a resolution. I shall walk with
her as if I wore the whole Sahara on my shoulder and there are three
lines together there: suddenly I know what I'm going to do and make
a whole picture so it's a solid block on the page. And then I go back
to being puzzled, and then I remember my mother and her mother:
the last three stanzas are all two lines each. In the second last stanza,
my mother says of her mother, 'the light shows through her, she is
full of holes,' and I've broken the line after 'full', because I'm doing
something to do with paradox, that I now understand much better
than I did when I wrote the poem. I wanted to say the light shows
through her, she is full, meaning she is full of light. But I also want
to say the light shows through her, she is full of holes so there are
holes and so the light can come through. I'm doing something to do
with what the gospels say about the poor shall inherit the earth and
the first shall be last, so that spiritual riches are material poverty,
so that's why I broke the line after 'she is full.' I could have put
'the light shows through her, [break] she is full of holes' but then
I wouldn't have got the idea she is full and also she is terribly
threadbare.

BH: This is something that, perhaps, is unique to poetry: that you can
actually have an intelligible unit, a clause, but because of where you
choose to break the line, you can introduce contrary meanings,

because people will see that little bit of the phrase by itself for a moment before they go on to the next line and they get the completion of the phrase, and so it allows for paradox; it allows for a secondary meaning to arise and then fall away.

GA: Yes, that's right. It makes it terribly hard to read aloud because you have to choose. I try not to choose, but it becomes complicated and you can never tell which of the two meanings people will arrive at, or whether they will, in fact, take in both, but then perhaps that depends on the readiness of their minds for any particular poem.

BH: I like that phrase, 'readiness of mind', because it seems that a lot of the things that you are discussing here are really about how the poem can present the mind and how lineation – as you say, having a whole stanza gap between lines, or bunching – how that can actually be a way of mapping and presenting a mind in, in action. I suppose, in order to be able to do that with confidence you really have to have readiness of mind, you have to be very alert to your own speech patterns, your own thought patterns. Is that one of the things which lineation can do?

GA: Yes, and also if you write in persona, it can help to present the voice of the person so that you are presenting the person not only in what you make them say, but in how you make them say it. My recent book, *Sojourner*, is, as I see it, full of extremely inarticulate people, in whose voices I have written poems.

BH: Now, we talked about complete sentences, we talked about breaking into the sentence. What about when we have actually a broken sentence, where the poem itself refuses to complete a sentence?

GA: My poems now refuse to complete the sentence much more than they did before. Something I've done a lot of in the last few years in workshops is go from lists to poems and you could argue that list items are already incomplete poems, sorry, incomplete sentences. [Laughter] That's actually what I'm puzzling my head over now: what the poems seem to be wanting to do now, is to say, 'No, not complete sentences any more, let's stop here in mid-air and see what happens.'

BH: That must be quite difficult for you, as a teacher who is presenting one rule to the class and who wants to keep with the class, then to discover yourself doing something different from that, breaking the rule, as it were.

GA: Yes, I've had to stop being quite so definite about writing in whole sentences. I have spent years haranguing classes as to why they think just because it's poetry they are allowed to write in incomplete sentences and leave out articles. But I hesitate before saying that now because I know that that's not what I'm doing myself. I have spent years going through my own apprenticeship, according to my own instructions and writing poems in whole sentences and thinking very hard about each time I don't do it, so I'm now going on from there and, although I feel as if I'm moving from the norm of whole sentences to a norm of fragments. It makes for huge problems of punctuation and I feel as if all my work at the moment is trying to sort out punctuation.

BH: Can you see why in your own work you are choosing consciously or unconsciously not to write in that way?

GA: To some extent, yes. I'm trying not to pre-empt reality, not to pre-empt what is.

> **Dottle, Donkey Man**
> Neither nephew nor niece.
> During the war, lowered the ride-price to a ha'penny.
> Ignored the world beyond the wire, as if sea only.
> On the mantelpiece, a small clay one, given him
> Glued together.
> Lived, as if among deaf men, alone,
> Dumb, like one walking into Jerusalem.

BH: It's not an inarticulacy, is it? It's a deliberate refraining, and the way that a poem can space things through lineation is part of almost affirming that decision to withdraw, withdrawing from a part of speech but also withdrawing from a certain attitude, an egocentric attitude. It's almost more powerful than a full sentence.

GA: Yes, it's almost in note form. And I think perhaps 'neither nephew nor niece' creates a greater sense of isolation than saying he had no nephews and no nieces, let alone children, or even just saying 'He had neither nephew nor niece,' which is a complete sentence. But he's gruff and unwilling to speak and he might have said 'No nephews, no nieces,' so I'm trying to almost put what I imagine what would have been his direct speech into indirect speech in a short opening line.

BH: Now that kind of progression is, I think, something that a new writer will work through or work towards, as you say, as they go through their apprenticeship. There are some devices that they might employ to help them get there, and I am just wondering whether these are devices that have much role in your writing. I am talking about things like counting the lines out syllabically or using alliteration as a way of balancing lines or indeed using rhyme as a way of closing lines.

GA: I never count syllables. I listen all the time when I am writing and I either say the growing lines aloud or I hear them in my head, all the time I'm writing. It's like dancing. And I do a lot of work on matching of sounds, alliteration, assonance, rhyme and half-rhyme and that again, it's more like dancing or making music.

BH: People sometimes think of these effects, particularly rhyme, obviously, as something which occurs at the end: it sort of ties the line together. But I think when you talk about alliteration and assonance you are really talking about something that's happening within the line and across the lines. So I'm just thinking about this notion of line as holding something in for the reader, whether that's the sentence or it's this dance, this music. Do you have a poem in which we can hear that sort of thing happening in relation to rhyme?

GA: Yes. Again, I'd like to relate writing to teaching. Another thing I spout perpetually is 'Don't rhyme' and 'Only rhyme if you absolutely must,' and I find this particularly when I'm working with children. When a child brings a poem and it's full of rhymes and everything is sacrificed to the rhyme, then I'll go through the poem and say, 'Do you really need this word at the end of this line?' and, 'Why did you choose that word?' and 'Shall we think of another one?' I usually use full rhyme for humour. I think it's probably true that I never use it, unless for humour. I really, really like half rhyme, and within a poem whose line endings are based on a pattern of half rhyme, there will be some full rhymes, but they can be so clunky you have to be very careful. But clunkiness is a gift if you are trying to use humour.

My Camberwell Grandmother Before Her Marriage
The upholsterer's late.
He'll say that he couldn't get over the road at New Cross Gate.
A little man from Mile End, moth-eaten,
Must have grown up on bread and gin,
How did Father get hold of him? I don't know.

I wish he had not. For now
There's no end to the mending of Mother's old chairs, the ones
She chose from Dickens & Jones.
I wish she'd gone out of this life
Like a light, like Elijah's wife
Herself, two flaming chairs, a double chariot of fire,
That's how I'd like to remember Mother.
Not as I now must, waiting in all afternoon. I might have been
In Worthing. Mother, of course, would be gone
To the corner of Jerningham Road
To choose bricks from the yard
For the outhouse Father began in nineteen hundred and six,
Mother loved choosing bricks.
I suppose they would meet, herself, the upholsterer,
Waiting to cross between motor-cars,
She'd notice the bodkin stuck in his hat,
She used to tell Father about it at night
In their room. *Did you notice*
The bodkin? she'd ask, undoing her bodice
And all those buttons, his buttons,
Her buttons of bone.

GA: Now I noticed towards the end of that poem that I read straight across the line-endings, the rhymes. But I read as she would have said it so that you don't notice the rhymes too much, although 'notice' and 'bodice' do come at the ends of the lines.

BH: This is a way of using lineation to almost bury the sounds, so that then there's a kind of muting. It means that they sort of pop up as slightly knobbly, button-like objects themselves, the rhymes when they happen.

GA: Yes. It's to have both the clunk and not to have the clunk of those end rhymes. I mean, it is a daft poem, but it's also saying something quite serious. I'm being extremely critical of my inheritance, my ancestors, my family, and partly I'm being critical by using ridiculous rhymes.

BH: One of the things you're doing in this poem is introducing quite a variety of short and long lines, each of which is bound by a rhyme, so that there's not an even rhythm, which relates back to what you've been saying. It's almost as though you are dancing around the notion of a formally exact measured unit: your work is aware of it, but that you never quite are prepared to go with it. I'm looking here for ways in which the actual structure of the poem reflects the mind and the personality of the person composing the poem and thinking about how new writers can seek this out in their own work.

GA: I actually really like using rhyming couplets because it's easy and it provides a very firm structure, a very strong rule to move around, so it's like having a simple 12-bar blues tune and improvising and really going to town on some of the variations.

BH: The issue that the alternation of long and short lines and the run over line where, as you say, you are almost concealing the rhyme . . . the issue that that raises for the reader is one of memorability. How distinct the units are that you are putting forth and whether they will lodge in the memory of the reader. Do you think of line as a unit of memorability in that way or is that something you resist?

GA: My ideal is that each line should mean in itself. That's a very strong basic principle, so that any line could be removed from the poem and mean something all by itself, although it will mean more and/or differently within the context of the poem. So if read with the line before it will mean one thing; read on its own it will mean another; read with the line following it, it will mean something else; and read with the line either side of it, perhaps something else again; within the whole poem something else again. And again that's like breaking the line so as to have two meanings instead of one. It's arranging the lines so that each one means by itself but means again in company, means differently in company with its fellows or means additionally.

BH: Obviously it's a matter of practice, endless practice, but the course you seem to be discussing, whereby a writer becomes sufficiently aware of what it is they are trying to say to map this into lines, are there guidelines you can offer them for that or is it simply, live with it and see?

GA: I did put myself through an apprenticeship of sorts in my mid-20s, when I gained enough confidence to take my writing seriously and notice that, if I worked on it, it actually went somewhere, it actually got better. I would advise people to try formal forms for the sake of what you learn from doing it. If you try to write a sonnet you understand something about why you have 14 lines in iambic pentameter in this particular rhyme scheme and you will, perhaps, take some notion about form and the way it serves contents from doing that.

BH: So, by going through it, you achieve a real freedom. When people are coming into it, they just think of freedom, they don't think of the constraint necessary to learn a more useful sense of freedom.

GA: Yes. I think, however I'm writing, usually about a third of the way into writing a poem, it will suggest its own form. It will say, no I don't want to be in three-line verses, I want to be in two-line verses and I'll go with that; and sometimes I'll realise I misheard it and maybe it wants to be in four-line verses, but it's a negotiation – I will welcome that hint of a rule and I think I usually set myself some sort of rule, so that I will have one sentence per line, or it's quite often a rule about punctuation: I'll try this poem entirely in lower case or I'll try it conventionally punctuated. And quite often I'll come to see a poem as a dance or a dialogue between two particular sounds. And, actually, lineation comes into that quite a lot because there'll quite often be one of those key sounds or both of them will come at the end of the lines.

BH: But lineation and punctuation are not that far apart because one of the uses of lineation which people come back to is as a kind of grand punctuation, a way of punctuating thoughts as well as grammar. So, there is a sense in which lineation is very much caught up with punctuating something. Do you ever let lineation stand in for punctuation in a poem and, if so, how effective is it at doing that?

GA: Yes, sometimes it's really interesting to see if I can use line breaks as my only form of punctuation. That's where I mentioned writing entirely in lower case, so that all I've got is line break and stanza break. That's a very extreme and difficult thing to do but it can be interesting to experiment with that as part of the process of writing and find out that, no, it's too restricting, so I'll allow myself some commas or dashes or whatever as well.

BH: It's testing it to destruction almost, isn't it? It's going for a purity which then you can step back from, in the interests of the poem.

GA: Yes, that's right. But I think it's impossible to write a poem without a rule of some kind while you are working. So, if it isn't a given rule or a set of rules like a sonnet has or a ballad or a sestina, then you have to invent something for the duration, at least that's what I do. I always do.

BH: Does that rule need to be apparent to the reader? I mean, the way that the rule of a sonnet is apparent – they can see that there's something going on there – is the rule something that can be internal, or must it be evident through the way the poem is presented or the way it comes over to the reader?

GA: I don't know. It would be interesting to give a poem of mine to a class and say, 'Can you see the rules by which I was writing this?' and see what happens. It could actually be a very good exercise because people are so often, so despairingly saying, 'It doesn't rhyme, why is it a poem, what makes it a poem?' Thank you, I might do that.

BH: A great difficulty that I think writers have in handling the process of writing is that you don't do everything for conscious reasons; you do a certain amount of things on trust, and learning how to trust yourself is really quite difficult. But, when it comes to lineation, it's overt: you really have to break the line somewhere, so how do you trust that?

GA: Whether you do this with a tutor or by yourself you need to ask about every single line ending. Why? Why here? Why here? Justify why you broke the line exactly where you did and not one word before or one word after.

BH: So the act of writing the poem becomes almost a self-interrogation or the poem interrogates you about its own procedure.

GA: I think the general pattern of writing a poem is to write it or let it write itself, and go with it, to do it intuitively; but the penultimate stage is to go through it with an absolute minute toothcomb and justify everything, including the line breaks. I frequently say to classes the one thing that I cannot teach you and no tutor can teach you is precisely that process of inner discrimination that is what writing a poem is about, and that you have to develop and learn to trust. You have to learn when something is profound and when it's just confused; when it's beyond your present comprehension and when it's totally muddled. You have to learn to know the difference and you can't ever completely know that you know the difference. Nobody but nobody can teach you that. It is interesting, this conversation, because I've never been aware, really, of how, in a way, it's a dance with the lines, it's reading across them and counter to them.

BH: The sense of the line has to be created for the dance to begin.

GA: Yes. I love improvising in music; I think that's what I'm doing when I write poems. I've never thought that before. But you've got to have a tune around which to improvise.

References

Allnutt, Gillian (2001) 'The Silk Light of Advent', in *Lintel*. Tarset: Bloodaxe Books, p. 24.

Allnutt, Gillian (2001), 'My Camberwell Grandmother before Her Marriage', in *Lintel*. Tarset: Bloodaxe Books, p. 22.

Allnutt, Gillian (2001) 'Child', in *Sojourner*. Tarset: Bloodaxe Books, p. 55.

Allnutt, Gillian (2001), 'Dottle, Donkey Man', in *Sojourner*. Tarset: Bloodaxe Books, p. 36.

Many prospective poets consider themselves to be searching for their voice, which is seen as a recognisable combination of tone and subject. Together with the primacy of inspiration and the successful first draft, voice is felt to be another trait of the 'proper' writer. Like those, it can have a counterproductive role in a writer's evolution. It is better to grow into a voice, and to keep that voice flexible, than to seek to fix it at the earliest opportunity.

Voice is something to be discovered rather than imposed, and it is rarely a single entity: some poets argue there are as many voices as there are poems. It's more practical to begin by identifying the voice of the individual poem we are working on, and to build from that a sense of the range of voices we can successfully use.

Activity 3.1   Reading

Read Richard Hugo on 'public and private poets', in an extract from *The Triggering Town* (1992: 14–15). Do you agree with these two categories?

> [. . .] Please don't take this too seriously, but for purposes of dis-
> cussion we can consider two kinds of poets, public and private.
> Let's use as examples Auden and Hopkins. The distinction (not a

valid one, I know, but good enough for us right now) doesn't lie in the subject matter. That is, a public poet doesn't necessarily write on public themes and the private poet on private or personal ones. The distinction lies in the relation of the poet to the language. With the public poet the intellectual and emotional contents of the words are the same for the reader as for the writer. With the private poet, and most good poets of the last century or so have been private poets, the words, at least certain keywords, mean something to the poet they don't mean to the reader. A sensitive reader perceives this relation of poet to word and in a way that relation – the strange way the poet emotionally possesses his vocabulary – is one of the mysteries and preservative forces of the art. With Hopkins this is evident in words like 'dappled,' 'stippled,' and 'pied.' In Yeats, 'gyre.' In Auden, no word is more his than yours.

Discussion

Which type of poet do you think you are? Whenever I am asked a question like this, I always say 'both' out of principle. Is it possible to be both types of poet at the same time? I would argue Walt Whitman is an example of this kind of writer, constantly reaching out to a whole nation, but in a language charged with inner meaning.

Hugo is asking you to focus on your relationship with language in a passionate way. Many people regard words as transparent means to an end: they contain a meaning, we speak or write the word containing the desired meaning, and that is the only meaning which is communicated. No account is taken of resonance, nuance or the irrational. I remember how I felt as a teenager when I first read Whitman's poem 'Eidolons' – I had no clear idea what an eidolon was, but it had a powerful effect, as though I was being shown a secret part of the mind – I almost didn't want to look the word up in a dictionary, in case it broke the spell. (It didn't: dictionaries are the biggest spell-books.)

Everyone has a way of speaking that's unique, and the same is true of how we write. Writers unaware of this produce an unusual mixture of styles: their work contains some unconsidered phrases which feel almost anonymous; and other phrases filled with – equally unconsidered – personal quirkiness. The former are things anyone would say, and indeed no one would notice. The latter are things only they would say, which only they can't hear. The search for a voice is often nothing more than bringing our attention to bear on how we already write, and filtering out that writing which conveys no individual charge.

Activity 3.2   Writing

Produce an alphabet of your favourite words. Twenty-six words which you find intriguing or delightful. They can be words from your childhood, words from the workplace, words from books. You can have loved them for years, or just be deciding to like them right now.

Here you might want to have recourse to an old writer's technique: it's called cheating. If when you get to a particular letter you can't think of a word that you like, go to the dictionary, open it at that letter, and put your finger down without looking. If you don't like that word, try the one above or below it. This relates to an old form of divination called the *sortes virgilianae* – people used to take their problems to Virgil's works, stick a finger in at random, and see if the quote helped them out.

Once you've assembled 26, ask yourself: 'Why did I pick this word?' Was it because of its sound or its sense? Only rarely will it be 50–50, more usually it's predominantly one or the other. But a writer's vocabulary must be a balanced unit, equally full of sound and sense. So pick another 26 words, and this time use the opposite category: if you picked 'abstract' because of its sense, pick 'abalone' because of its sound, and vice versa.

Now let's construct a simple acrostic: take the letters of your first name, and run them down the left-hand column of a page. Mine would be:

B
I
L
L

Take your choices for each letter of your name. (As you can see, for mine I would have to find two more favourites beginning with 'l'.) Write a sentence for each letter, which must contain the two words. Keep it relatively brief, so there's a chance of picking up its rhythm, and try to make it make sense, but don't worry too much about that. See if you can count the number of beats it contains, but don't worry about regularising these.

This exercise generates a strange kind of self-portrait: it builds a picture of you out of letters and words, all of which are more or less intimately connected to you. Is it therefore in your 'voice'? Of course not, but there may be turns of phrase that strike you as characteristic. Note these. If there aren't any, do the same for your surname, or pick a theme word, a hobby you like, for instance 'bowling' or 'ikebana' (flower arranging), and do the same for that.

Notice I haven't asked you to make connections between each of the sentences, or indeed between all of the sentences and the name which forms the acrostic. You are of course at liberty to do so, but consider this: your voice is not just built up of what you say, it is also composed of what you don't say, the pauses or leaps between sentences or topics. Which feels right for you?

You may feel that poetic voice is something much more to do with tone or subject matter. But poets tend to be literal creatures when it comes to language: your voice, whatever it is, is made of specific words in specific combinations. My suggestion is: find the words, then look for the combinations. So pick a word summing up a tone you're after, or a subject – say 'licentious' or 'Luddite' – and try to explore that tone or subject in the sentences you construct.

This exercise creates a set of laboratory conditions where all these issues can be explored. Start keeping a record of changes to your favourite words: over a period of time it may settle down to Hugo's 'words you can own'.

The search for a voice is not something that will be resolved in the duration of this book, or even in years of writing. Sometimes the discovery of something we can classify as our voice coincides with a weariness with that voice, and the struggle begins to create a new voice. But the act of searching, concentrating as it does on reading and listening to our work, considering our feelings about words and tone with greater intensity, tunes our instrument, language, and polishes our technique.

Idiolect

Each of us clearly has an idiolect, a particular way of speaking derived from our upbringing and education. Our parents' and relatives' speech patterns and vocal tics and mannerisms; the way people speak where we were born; the way people speak where we live now; what we've read and when we read it: all these feed in to the way we unconsciously select one expression over another, one rhythm or one word as opposed to another. Poetry enables us to become as conscious as possible about the nuances of language, indeed to manipulate those elements to an aesthetic end.

For some writers, the task is to remain as authentic to those patterns as possible; for others, their idiolect is the basic template they will manipulate or even step away from to create new modes of expression. You will explore your voice to decide which tactic is right for which poem.

Michael Longley states:

> Poetry is mainly about putting the right word in the right place, a question of rhythm more than anything else. The ideal choice of word also decides tone of voice and verbal colour. This is where the idiomatic nature of English is invaluable. We can further enrich the argot by turning to dialect, though as one who speaks fairly standard English I would only do so when the dialect of my region, Ulster Scots, sets free a concept or phrase or line which would otherwise not be accessible to me.
>
> (Longley 1996: p. 115)

Notice how for Longley there is no sense that one type of language is superior to another. In creative terms there is no debate about whether one form of speech is 'proper' and another 'improper', there is only an issue about how naturally the language will fit in the poem in question.

You might like to have a look at that list of favourite words. Are any of them words which are local to your area or even family words like Paul Muldoon's term for a hot-water bottle, 'quoof' (we'll look at his poem of this name in Activity 5.5)? If there's another language spoken in your home, are there words in that language which are used even when speaking English? Are any words there because they are used by your favourite writers?

Activity 3.3   Reading

Now read શેરડી (Shérdi) by Sujata Bhatt, from New British Poetry (2004 [1998]: 21–2). Do you feel her introduction of non-English terms is subtle or intrusive?

शेरડી *(Shérdi)*

The way I learned
to eat sugar cane in Sanosra:
I use my teeth
to tear the outer hard *chaal*
then, bite off strips
of the white fibrous heart –
suck hard with my teeth, press down
and the juice spills out.

January mornings
the farmer cuts tender green sugar cane
and brings it to our door.
Afternoons, when the elders are asleep
we sneak outside carrying the long smooth stalks.
The sun warms us, the dogs yawn,
our teeth grow strong
our jaws are numb;
for hours we suck out the *russ*, the juice
sticky all over our hands.
So tonight
when you tell me to use my teeth,
to suck hard, harder,
then, I smell sugarcane grass,
in your hair
and imagine you'd like to be
shérdi shérdi out in the fields
the stalks sway
opening a path before us

शेरડी (Shérdi): sugar cane

Discussion

Sujata Bhatt cleverly plays intimacy off against what is, for some of us, an exotic setting. Notice how she places Gujarati before English and only glosses the title at the end of the poem. So there is a parallel between the delayed revelation of her sensual subject matter and the revelation (for an English-speaking audience) of her language. This delay is reflected in the choice whether or not to gloss words in the text: '*chaal*' is not glossed, while, later on, '*russ*' is. Of course, drawing out this line by adding this gloss also contributes towards the languorous atmosphere of the poem: 'for hours we suck out the *russ*, the juice.'

Despite this sophisticated layering of language, the tone of this poem is conversational until the lyric shift in the final part, where the repetition of the title takes on an incantatory feel. She convinces us that this mixture of language is entirely natural, even when she's clearly manipulating it towards her aesthetic end.

How natural do you think the voice we encounter in poetry should sound? What about a writer like Tom Leonard who abandons conventional spelling in order to represent the voice of a particular city and class? Are there certain ways of speaking that you personally find less suitable? Do you feel that it is part of the poet's task to present the best of the language?

These are not leading questions. Decorum – finding the most suitable language for a given poem – is an important standard for the poet to pursue. Our notion of what is natural or appropriate, however fraught, forms an inevitable part of the process of composition.

Can we always say a poem should sound natural in the sense that all of its language should appear as the ordinary idiolect of whoever we imagine to be speaking the poem? But what if there isn't a definite, single speaker of the poem? What if the speaker is a robot or an antelope? What if the speaker is a herd of robot antelope?

The issue of idiolect and the associated matter of finding a suitable register for a poem are very like the issue of finding a voice. They open us to a sense of the astonishingly diverse ways of writing at our disposal, some of which may well not sound particularly natural, some of which resoundingly will. The real issue remains: are they effective, and if so, what is that effect? Is it, as Michael Longley concludes, something that could not have been achieved by any other means?

Activity 3.4   Writing

Write for 10 minutes about an incident from your childhood where you were the centre of attention. It could be the time a relative showed you how to cook or garden; it could be a short performance you put on of your sporting or musical prowess. Write about what happened, where it happened, how everyone reacted.

Then write for a further 10 minutes about that incident from the point of view of the relatives or neighbours who witnessed it. See if there are any terms or modes of expression they would use but you would not. See if they would notice different things about what happened or its implications.

The exploration of idiolect is an exploration of resources. It is not incumbent on you to discover or learn a lost language, or to choose to write in the other language spoken in your family, or to put on an accent in your poetry that you wouldn't be comfortable speaking. But it is important that your poetry is not built out of a partial model of the range of Englishes and other languages that make up your linguistic consciousness.

Personae

Poetry is not always about self-expression in the sense that the 'I' who speaks in the poem is always the 'I' of the poet. Sometimes giving voice to others can be the most effective way we can find of expressing what we want to say. That other voice can be our polar opposite or a historical personage; it can be a character from someone else's fiction or even an object. Some poets have found that finding and fully inhabiting these other voices becomes the driving principle of their poetry.

By exploring the range of voices we can inhabit, we gain insights into ourselves. Sometimes we even gain insights into the constructed nature of the voice we employ when we attempt to speak as ourselves.

Activity 3.5   Reading

Read Edwin Morgan in interview on this issue (Edwin Morgan (1990) *Nothing Not Giving Messages: Reflections on work and life*. Hamish Whyte (ed.). Edinburgh: Polygon, pp.130–1).

> *Your 1973 collection is called* From Glasgow to Saturn. *Your selected translations carry the title* Rites of Passage. *The idea of constant translation – linguistic, cultural, and geographic – seems central to your work as a whole. Do you feel that that's the case?*

Translation in all senses! Well, maybe so. I like translation itself as an activity, the challenge of translation, of trying to do it as well as I can [. . .] the whole business of communication – I suppose that comes into translation – always interested me a lot and it was partly the difficulties of communication (I suppose that's often a theme in what I write) or even imaginary communication, but again the idea of bringing things together and of giving things a voice through what I write, even if they don't have an actual voice – giving animals or inanimate objects a voice – that attracts me a lot, and I suppose that is a kind of translation in a way. If I write a poem called 'The Apple's Song', the apple is being translated if you like into *human* language. Who knows what an apple thinks! We don't really know – it doesn't give signs of thinking, but because we don't get signs of what an animal or a plant or a fruit really is thinking, I don't think we're entitled to just switch off and say it's not feeling or thinking. I like the idea particularly that in a sense we're surrounded by messages that we perhaps ought to be trying to interpret. I remember in 'The Starlings in George Square' I brought in the bit about 'Someday we'll decipher that sweet frenzied whistling', which in a sense I suppose I believed actually – although it seems just a fantastic idea.

Messages from the past and the future also?

I think probably also. Yes, yes, yes. The writer or the poet being in *receipt*, if you like, of messages, just like people listening for stars' messages, astronomers listening for that. I think the writer too does that kind of thing. He does his best. He tries to decode, if you like, the messages that he thinks he gets from everything that surrounds him. Nothing is not giving messages, I think.

Now read Jo Shapcott's 'The Mad Cow Talks Back', from *Phrase Book* (1992: 41). Imagine a world in which literally everything had a voice: would it drive you as mad as Jo Shapcott's cow?

The Mad Cow Talks Back

I'm not mad. It just seems that way
because I stagger and get a bit irritable.
There are wonderful holes in my brain
through which ideas from outside can travel

at top speed and through which voices,
sometimes whole people, speak to me
about the universe. Most brains are too
compressed. You need this spongy
generosity to let the others in.

I love the staggers. Suddenly the surface
of the world is ice and I'm a magnificent
skater turning and spinning across whole hard
Pacifics and Atlantics. It's risky when
you're good, so of course the legs go before,
behind, and to the side of the body from time
to time, and then there's the general embarrassing
collapse, but when that happens it's glorious
because it's always when you're travelling
most furiously in your mind. My brain's like
the hive: constant little murmurs from its cells
saying this is the way, this is the way to go.

Discussion

Some of you may have expected to get Browning's 'Last Duchess' at this point. But that poem can make us think that adopting the voice of a persona is essentially a dramatic action; that your character has to have almost Shakespearean or at least novelistic stature. What Morgan is arguing is that voice is a way of perceiving and interpreting the world, and that the range of personae open to us is extraordinarily diverse, something only bound by our sense of empathy. Real and imaginary people, yes, but also animals and inanimate objects.

Jo Shapcott's poem isn't exactly a dramatic monologue by a character you can imagine meeting. The Mad Cow isn't simply a cow with BSE; she is also readable as a woman, and as a kind of allegorical figure, though she doesn't 'stand' unambiguously for Progress or The Dangers of Progress. She requires us to extend our idea of what the poetic voice can contain, which is what I was hinting at above when I said that 'natural' wasn't always a useful concept to describe diction. The cow speaks like a sensible, literate woman, but she embodies something that goes beyond both sanity and the human.

So when you explore personae, I suggest you start with an animal or an object. It can be good to start with the non-human, for the simple reason that it forces our attention onto issues of voice. It's hard to do an impersonation of an apple, whereas most of us would have a set response if we were asked to become a musketeer. The object obliges us to think as far as possible without preconceptions.

Activity 3.6   Writing

Earlier, in Activity 2.3, I asked you to write about an animal; and, in Activity 1.1, I gave you the option of writing in the voice of an object from a postcard. You can go back to one of these and revise them in the light of the following instructions, or you can choose another animal or another object.

If you opt for the latter, pick an animal you've observed recently, perhaps a dog that is frequently walked past your house, or a cat whose territory you appear to be in. It could be a bird or other creature you've seen out of your window. (One night I opened my window to watch a ship go down the Tyne, and saw that there was a fox loping along the deserted road. The streetlights seemed to bleach all the colour out of it, and I noticed that it was running with a limp.)

If you pick an object, why not select one already in your house, perhaps something you've not looked at for a while, or even neglected? Garden furniture can work as well as kitchen implements; old souvenirs have as much to say as items of clothing.

Write for 15 minutes in the voice of this animal or this object. Consider how it might sound: a hacksaw might make a wheedling noise, full of 's's and fricatives. Think about how it might construct its speech: would an onion's sentences be full of parentheses, one inside another? Imagine what it most wants to say: would that bottle of untouched plum brandy be like the genie in the Arabian Nights, its early eagerness replaced by bitterness after years of neglect?

Discussion

How different was the voice you achieved in the last exercise to your own voice? Writing in voices is a way of looking back at ourselves. Sometimes we reveal more, catch more of a tone we recognise, by trying to go away from that voice. Sometimes not writing in our own voice helps us to define what that voice must therefore be.

The 'I' who appears in your poems is both intimately like and radically unlike you. It is a construct in the same way a poem in the voice of an onion is a construct. You can make it as like you as possible but, due to your selectivity and your invention, and the fact you're always creating a version of events, it's not exactly you. That doesn't make it a dramatic character exactly, but it means you can analyse this persona with the same degree of distance with which you analysed the object or the animal.

Narrative and other discourses

For most of literary history, poetry has been a way of telling stories. The lyric poem, in which a voice, more or less identified with the poet, appears to speak about experiences in the life of that poet, is just one form among many. When a story is told in verse, there is room to step away from this kind of verisimilitude and explore the act of storytelling. This may result in a narrative that feels less plot-driven than prose fiction, one that can experiment with pace or conventions of realism. Or it may result in the pared-down, super-real narration that we associate with ballads.

There are other ways of approaching the poetic act, some of which have a lineage extending over thousands of years, others being more the product of the last century's radical change and experimentation. Verse has been used to write about the nature of the universe; it has been written to appear on public art; and it has been collaged from the writing of others. Every mode should be examined for its possible expressiveness, and each way your voice can be extended should be examined.

In this section of the chapter we will look firstly at narrative in verse, and then experiment with moving away from conventional lyric subjects.

Activity 3.7   Reading

Read 'A Peculiar Suicide' by Matthew Sweeney, from *Cacti* (1992: 13). Consider the implications of this narrative: what are we not being told?

> **A Peculiar Suicide**
> Begin with the note left on the table,
> saying 'You'll never find me',
> in a ring of photographs of sons.

Ask the moustached, diving policeman
how many river-holes he searched
where the salmon spawn in glaur.

Ask colleagues, ask the long one
who searched the farm – he'll tell you
he found nothing bar the note.

Ask the neighbour who played dominoes,
as usual, with him in the bar
the night before he disappeared,

and who saw the spade was missing
from its usual place, and got
the assembled police wondering why.

Got them scouring the grassland
around the house, until finally
they found it, and freshly laid sods

hiding planks and a bin-lid
with a rope attached, and a tunnel
that didn't go very far.

Ask what they found at the end –
just him, and the pill jar,
and the coldest hot-water bottle of all.

Discussion

As elsewhere in Sweeney's poetry, this is a macabre account of what happened to an anonymous protagonist. His poetry can also be full of names, particularly place names, and its register is carefully assembled to suggest setting, often his native Donegal (notice the muddy Celtic word 'glaur'). But frequently the subject of his poems remains nameless, so we feel that we are being let into an account of awful events as outsiders, bystanders suddenly being given a shocking confidence. This is as deliberate a narrative device as Kafka telling us only the initial of his protagonist: K.

The genre this poem most resembles with its missing spade is the murder mystery – notice the instructions: 'Begin . . . Ask . . . Ask . . .'. We are drawn into the search for clues and encouraged to speculate about the elements we aren't given. Why has the man committed suicide? What has it to do with the 'ring of photographs of sons', for instance? But this is like the misdirection of the magician, and when teaching this poem I sometimes find myself reminding people: 'How did the suicidal man lay the sods after he'd put the bin-lid down?'

It is indeed a 'peculiar' suicide, and most of the peculiarity is generated by what the poet chooses to leave out, and how he focuses in like a tracking shot, finishing on that striking image, 'the coldest hot-water bottle of all'.

Activity 3.8 Writing

Think of the most unusual thing that's happened to you in recent weeks, or something odd that you've witnessed or someone has reported to you. If you've been keeping your notebook going, then you should have plenty such incidents to hand. Another resource is the newspaper or Internet, which is continually reporting small 'human interest' stories.

If you can't think of anything, here are a couple of examples, one domestic, the other outré – it's better to think of these as the kinds of thing to look for: only use them as a last resort.

Once when I was teaching this exercise in a school near Falkirk, one of the pupils told the class how one morning she had seen her neighbour get into her car whilst her cat was sleeping on the bonnet. She drove off to work and neither neighbour nor cat noticed – immediately – what was happening.

This article was torn out of a newspaper and inserted into my copy of *Cacti*:

> Police in central Shaanxi province arrested two brothers-in-law for digging up the corpses of two women last year and selling them as 'ghost brides' to the family of two men who died unmarried.

Write about your incident for 15 minutes, recounting it as though it were part of a longer narrative. Keep it in third person (he or she) and concentrate on detail. Speculate about the motive for what's happening, and what might have happened just before and just after it. Now select which part you're going to focus on. Will it be the incident or its projected aftermath?

Rewrite the piece cutting out as much of the motivation as possible and just focusing on that event. Search for the details which make telling the reader about motivation irrelevant. Remember you can keep it mysterious. (Handy if you can't work it out yourself!) Give yourself another 15 minutes on this, then make the usual notes preparatory to revision.

As I said earlier, the poetic voice isn't simply lyrical or narrative. We'll now examine some very different approaches to subject matter and genre.

Look at this grid of the classical muses.

Name	Meaning of Name	Domain	Symbols
Calliope	The Fair Voiced	Epic Poetry	Writing Tablet
Clio	The Proclaimer	History	Scroll
Erato	The Lovely	Love Poetry	Lyre
Euterpe	The Giver of Pleasure	Music	Flute
Melpomene	The Songstress	Tragedy	Tragic Mask
Polyhymnia	She of Many Hymns	Sacred Poetry	Pensive Look
Terpsichore	The Whirler	Dancing	Dancing with Lyre
Thalia	The Flourishing	Comedy	Comic Mask
Urania	The Heavenly	Astronomy	Celestial Globe

The muses were the daughters of Apollo (intellect) and Mnemosyne (memory) – an interesting parentage for inspiration.

Modern culture has laid some solid barriers across the field of activity the Greeks would have recognised as the muses' domain. Astronomy is now considered a science, but should that mean the heavens need no longer inspire poetry? Not many people would regard themselves as writing 'sacred poetry' these days, though poets as different as R.S. Thomas, John Burnside and Pauline Stainer can be described as doing exactly that. And who writes historical poems or epics any more? (Well, Tom Paulin and Derek Walcott for two.)

Our society's conception of poetry is still largely shaped by a notion of the personal lyric – what the Greeks might see as Erato's territory – with a dash of tragedy in the mix for seriousness' sake. Births, (four) weddings and funerals are the points when we traditionally turn to verse, and the verse we traditionally turn to is what we half-digested at school – a Shakespeare sonnet, Wordsworth on daffodils, Masefield at sea – hearts, flowers and the lonely heavens. And yet for centuries poets have been writing about everything under and in those heavens in the widest possible variety of ways.

It can be good to shake our voice loose a little from dwelling on our immediate surroundings and our feelings. And it might help to have nine types of inspiration rather than (infrequently) one.

Activity 3.9   Writing

Write for 20 minutes on four or five occasions in which you could be regarded as encountering any of the muses. Interpret this rubric as generously or as cynically as you see fit. For instance, we all had a brush with Urania when they announced the discovery of Sedna, the tenth planet. You may not have seen much contemporary dance lately, but when was the last time you stood up suddenly (perhaps leaving a hostelry) and experienced 'The Whirler'? Would you like to invent a tenth muse? Should she be the muse of cookery or gardening? Pay particular attention to the type of language you encounter in these different fields of interest.

Discussion

Types of the introspective lyric still fill most of the poetry books you will read, and it may be the case that your work too will tend to fall largely into this category. But the poetic imagination has always been capable of approaching the world from a number of different angles. Borrowing from the novel or the film, it can tell stories with intensity, strangeness or humour. By considering its own larger heritage, it can adopt and adapt other discourses, approaching different subject matters from love and despair, or bring those other areas to bear on traditional lyric concerns.

Keep your voice as open as your eyes, ears and notebook.

References

Bhatt, Sujata (2004 [1998]) 'Shérdi', in Don Paterson and Charles Simic (eds) *New British Poetry*. Saint Paul, Minn.: Graywolf.

Hugo, Richard (1979) *The Triggering Town: Lectures and essays on poetry and writing*. New York and London: W.W. Norton & Company.

Leonard, Tom (1995) *Intimate Voices: Selected work 1965–1983*. London: Vintage.

Longley, Michael (1996) 'A Tongue at Play', in Tony Curtis (ed.), *How Poets Work*. Bridgend: Seren.

Shapcott, Jo (1992) 'The Mad Cow Talks Back', in *Phrase Book*. Oxford: Oxford University Press.

Sweeney, Matthew (1992) 'A Peculiar Suicide', in *Cacti*. London: Secker & Warburg.

Part 2

Dialogue: Kathleen Jamie (KJ) and Bill Herbert (BH)

BH: I think that when people start with the notion of the voice they think that is the goal. That is the thing that they are heading for. So I was wondering if you had ever experienced that as a realisation: that you had a voice, or was it something that was imposed on you? That people told you that you had a voice?

KJ: I think the business of voice, it's a young person's problem. And when you – I mean by that when students have in my experience been anxious about finding their voice and sometimes it becomes just laughable, although obviously you don't laugh. And they say, 'Yes. I want to be a writer but I can't find my voice.' And I feel like saying, 'Look down behind the sofa. Most things are there.' And it's a bit of a myth. In fact it's a complete myth, that there is a voice and when once attained you will go on through the next 60 years of your writing life without let or hindrance. I think it comes from the idea that poetry is oracular and all you have to do is tune in to this voice within yourself and then just speak and everything will be fine. So it's a way of avoiding the learning process, learning the craft and the skills of poetry, it skirts around that. When you have achieved this voice a whole lot of other problems come in. In my own work I have discovered I have had a voice and the minute I have thought, 'Oh, I have got that voice,' that's when the project ends. That's not the beginning of the project, it's the end, because you become self-conscious and self-aware of writing in that voice and then everything you do thereafter is just parodying yourself. There is also the problem of tribalism. If you are let us say a woman or you are let us say black or gay or whatever, if you have these sort of issues to negotiate around, you can sometimes be expected to write in the voice of a woman, a black person, a gay person or whatever and that weight of expectation can limit you or damage you and it can mean that you feel you have to adopt this voice and write in it and if you stop doing that you can feel that you are betraying your people. And you can be told in no uncertain terms that you are betraying your people. So voice is a curious, curious thing. It's not altogether a good thing to pursue. It's not altogether a good thing to attain.

BH: There is a kind of counter notion that each poem has its own voice and I sometimes wonder whether that is a kind of splintered version of the same oracular notion. You know, that instead of you having the voice the poem has the voice.

KJ: I have got more patience with that, that it works poem by poem and each poem you are constructing you have to make the voice that will carry it.

BH: Well, let's talk about that because the constituency thing, the tribal thing, takes us right on into what the nuts and bolts of a voice might be. I mean if it is not the god or goddess speaking then obviously there has to be stuff that is simply part of the world of language that you have grown up through or grown up with. How do you feel about the notion that voice is a kind of accretion, it's a kind of life process, like trees putting on rings, and it is to do with where you have been and where you have come from. Do you think that relates to a poetic voice?

KJ: Very strange image of a tree covered in lichen now. Do you mean as we grow as poets?

BH: Yes. I have this vision of the tree that if you cut right through it and you get that ring right through the whole thing then you see where your voice came from at each point – and then you put the tree ring on to the record player and it plays you a lovely tune.

KJ: Well it seems to me that we are kind of just stuck then, and you have no control or no sway over it. The older I get the more I realise that you can actually control it, because voice is just made up of constituent parts and as you learn to adapt and control each of these you can change your voice. So it's not coming from some sacred well within. You can actually change it if you want to. Just decide not to write like that anymore.

BH: So you can write against the grain of an upbringing, for instance?

KJ: Absolutely. Maybe have to sometimes. I mean it causes all sorts of inner tensions but I don't think we need to be stuck, governed, by the place we came from. You have to work through it, and it can take 20 years to reach a place where you think, 'I have done that now and now I can go and try and work with different voices and different ideas.' I am not eternally stuck being the same wee girl from Currie or whatever. And you learn, as you learn the craft and techniques of poetry, you learn how to change your voice just by changing – *just by* – listen to her – by changing the diction or the syntax of the register.

BH: I am thinking about the 'whae do you think you are?' voice in 'The Queen of Sheba' or the 'forget it' voice where you have these admonishing voices from the past, where you feel that the effort of the imagination is to struggle to contain them and yet to free yourself from them as well.

KJ: Bring them into the fold and annul them in a way – bringing them in annuls them. I have lost all patience with that kind of writing actually. I haven't heard any of the pop-up voices for a long time and if I have I just ignore them now.

BH: They seem to me though to relate a little bit to the way that you use stories in your work. There is a strain of allusion to figures – The Queen of Sheba would be a classic figure – but before that the princess who breaks the sun-moon mirror in that earlier sequence, or I remember you talking about the ballad 'Tam Linn' as a metaphor for writing. I was just thinking about the way that those voices and those stories are impinging on the lyric concerns. There are narratives out there that are waiting to get you, as it were.

KJ: Isn't it a flaming nuisance? Don't you wish they would go away and shut up and let you get on with it? And then get back to this pure voice idea. If it wasn't for all this racket in your head you would have this wonderful pure voice.

BH: Well, that's like sitting here and not expecting any cars to go by or the planes to take off from Leuchars. It's the soundscape that the poems take place in.

KJ: Shutting them out, excluding them. Just telling them to go away for a wee while because you are concentrating. You get fed up with that kind of intrusion. And I am mistrustful of voices. I am mistrustful of working in voices because I sometimes think it's an evasion. It means you have not been brave enough to think about what really wants to be thought about. Do you know those families that pass difficult remarks through their pet? Do you know what I mean? Dog's called Ben and, 'Ben thinks you are misbehaving' means, 'I think you are misbehaving but I can't say that to you so I have to route it through the dog.' And I think that the poems in other voices do that. Route difficult things and make it possible to see them by routing them through this third party. And I think it's braver now to try and do it directly. But it's a very great asset for a writer to have all these other people and animals available to do that routing.

BH: So one of the things that I feel that people are constantly asking of a teacher of poetry is the rule, you know, they are trying to find The Rule and they have a sense that there is going to be a few of these that will govern them; that will carry them through. And of course the problem is that there are no rules. There are only tendencies, there are only sorts of approaches, and this given sort of approach doesn't work every time. You have got to look at each problem afresh.

KJ: Ah the rule. The rule of course is there are no rules. There are no solutions only attitudes. But the idea of voice is a useful one I suppose to get young writers started and going, given the idea that there is this thing that they can tune into which is their own voice and if they can't find it, it doesn't really exist. If they can't find it they can use the voice of something else. There is no harm in that.

BH: So yes, personae and the idea I think that comes through in your last book that there are voices coming from things.

KJ:

> **The Cupboard**
> As for this muckle
> wooden cupboard carted hither
> years ago, from some disused
> branch-line station, the other
> side of the hill, that takes up
> more room than the rest of us
> put together, like a dour
> homesick whale, or mute sarcophagus –

> why is it at *my* place?
> And how did it sidle
> Through the racked,
> too narrow door, to hunker
> below these sagging rafters,
> no doubt for evermore?

BH: I think this relates to the way that you use ballads. I mean they are like ballads and they are not like ballads. It's like you are alluding to a territory that you are occupying in your work.

KJ: This is fascinating, the difference. I am very hostile to the idea – what you are hostile to you are usually hostile to because it is getting near the truth, isn't it? Personally I am sick and fed up of reading poems in the voice of a turnip; a pair of shoes – give us a break. I do think it's evasive.

BH: But I think that some of these objects are maybe totemic – so that they are enabling you to get to a voice.

KJ: Hopefully yes. Otherwise there is no blinking point in writing this stuff, is there? That's a very good function. And what is the point? The point is to do what? To get to the heart of something, to get to the truth of something by a long route. If you can't manage it by the short cut, the direct route, you have got to wander around the houses and make this kind of utterance that you couldn't make in your own voice – 'own voice' in quotes. You have got to animate something else and make it speak for you like a blinking ventriloquist's dummy. It's too silly for words actually.

BH: When I get impatient I think I want to throw out all the toys and I want to find a new way of saying anything. So I suppose that is an endeavour to lose the voice. Do you think that's possible?

KJ: You ditch the unfashionable ones – the ones that don't fit you any longer. Yes. As I said before if you keep on working in the same voice once you are aware of how to make that voice and it has been successful for you and you get plaudits for it; if you keep on working in that voice you are just impounding yourself, and it is time to think again because that project, whatever it was, is over. Whatever that voice was required for is now done. The voice is done as well.

BH: So it's like a sloughing of skins then?

KJ: Yes. I don't think they sit in a cupboard to be re-animated when required. Sometimes I look at older pieces of work I think, 'Oh that's nice. I wish I could write like that again.' But no – you won't. Nor should you. Every new poem, every new project – I am old enough now to think in projects, book-length projects – requires you take yourself apart almost at a cellular level and build yourself up again as a poet and the voice is one of those things that has to be constructed out of minuscule parts until you find the voice that is right for the project that you want to do. And it animates the material that you have and everything comes together for this glorious short period and then it all falls apart again.

BH: Do you think of the voice as a particularly significant part of the new endeavour?

KJ: I don't think of it at all to tell you the truth. I don't think of it as a constituent part because I can see it in its constituent parts. I don't fret about diction, I don't fret about syntax or fret about this and that, and those things combined arrive at something called 'Voice'.

BH: But there has to be a slight deliberation on your part because you write some poems that are actually in Scots and in a more marked way than a few words here and there you know. There is a kind of conscious decision . . .

KJ: Now that's different. That's language.

BH: Ah but, there is a decision about the voice which is being made there . . .

KJ: No. There is a decision about language. Language is not voice, is it? Regardless of which language you are working in you still have to go through the same business of constructing a voice for each poem. I wrote this poem in a very far away place, actually in China, and because the name of the Chinese term sounded to my ear like a Scots name I began thinking about my own Scots background which I had never written in before, so the first poem I wrote in Scots I actually wrote far away in China.

Xiahe

Abune the toon o Xiahe
a thrast monstery,
warn lik a yowe's tuith.

The sun gawps at innermaist
ingles o wa's.
Secret as speeders

folk hae criss-crosst a sauch
seedit i the yird flair
wi rags o win blawn prayer.

Xiahe. Wave droonin wave
on a pebbly shore,
the *ahe* o machair, o slammach,

o impatience; ahent the saft saltire
i trashed, and sheep;
wha's drift on the brae

is a lang cloud's shadda.
the herd cries a wheen wirds
o Tibetan sang,

an A'm waukenet, on a suddenty mindit:
A'm far fae hame,
I hae crossed China.

BH: So is there a decision for instance about vocabulary and there will be a certain amount of words that your granny knew or not?

KJ: Well, in every poem that you write you are thinking all the while about vocabulary, and the way it is constructed, and the forms the stanzas are going to take, and how much silence is built into it and the register, the tone of voice, the intimacy, how close you are speaking. Whether you are dropping words into someone's ear or whether you are bellowing at them through a tannoy. Those decisions. And what all those different things amount to is what we would likely call 'Voice'. So. Where does that leave us? I am thinking about the students who fret that they are not finding their voice.

BH: I think that what it leaves us with is a kind of reassurance. What you are saying is that the process of writing a poem takes care of the business of finding the voice.

KJ: It's a matter of not seeing the wood for the trees then. Yes. Maybe you are right. I did tell them not to worry about it. The voice is what you get when the poem is – it's just there. It's done. Once you have worried about everything else the voice just naturally arises in it.

BH: Nobody ever stops worrying about something just because you tell them not to worry about it!

KJ: The thing about this business of voice is we think that poetry is speaking. Speaking is about utterance and speech, which is why most people get into poetry. They get into it to speak, and then it becomes a terrible anxiety about finding the voice in which you have to speak, and having other people listen to your speech, which can then be a personal speech of your individual self which is one of the reasons people get hung up on it when they are young, when they are searching for their own individuality. Or it can become the speech of the tribe; whether that it is an ethnic tribe or gender tribe or whatever – you get pressurised if you are a poet to speak for the tribe. But lately, now that I am turned forty I am starting to rethink these things. I think it's more about listening. It's about listening to the world and in order to start listening properly you have to shut up speaking for a while. So just listening to the world, listening to the natural world, say, which is what I have been doing lately, involves shutting down all these different voices and not letting them get in, and understanding that they are nothing but evil. To listen properly meant cleansing my mind as best I could of all these egotistical interruptions, which are voices that wanted to be heard. And so the poems that I have been writing lately have no voice because the voice was merely intrusive and got in the way of the listening and that is what I am thinking about now.

References

Jamie, Kathleen (2004) 'The Cupboard', in *The Tree House*. London: Picador, p. 44.

Jamie, Kathleen (2004) 'Xiahe', in *Dream State: The New Scottish Poets*, ed. Donny O'Rourke. Edinburgh: Polygon. 2nd ed. pp.191–2.

4

Imagery

Part 1

The image appears to be a primary component both of language and indeed of how we conceptualise our world. We are constantly comparing one thing to another, or considering an idea as though it were a thing. As you'll see, many words and phrases are inherently metaphoric, and the imagery in others is clear enough from examining the roots of the word. 'Nostril', for example, combines 'nose' with 'thirl', or piercing, an old term for a window. So the nostril is the nose's window.

The image, then, is one point at which the practice of the poet would appear to be derived fairly naturally from universal habits. This makes it a powerful communicative tool.

Images can be used to familiarise the reader with unknown or exotic phenomena. Another perhaps more fruitful use for the image is to defamiliarise the overly familiar, to re-present the world to us as though we have never seen it before. In both cases it expands the range of our experience.

Activity 4.1   Reading

Read the extract from Julian Jaynes's *The Origin of Consciousness in the Breakdown of the Bicameral Mind* (1993, London: Penguin Books, pp. 48–51).Were you aware of this many instances of imagery cropping up in your everyday conversation? Does it make you think of others?

Metaphor and Language

It is by metaphor that language grows. The common reply to the question 'what is it?' is, when the reply is difficult or the experience unique, 'well, it is like –.' [. . .] This is the major way in which the vocabulary of language is formed. The grand and vigorous function of metaphor is the generation of new language as it is needed, as human culture becomes more and more complex.

A random glance at the etymologies of common words in a dictionary will demonstrate this assertion. Or take the naming of various fauna and flora in their Latin indicants, or even in their wonderful common English names, such as stag beetle, lady's slipper, darning needle, Queen Anne's lace, or buttercup. The human body is a particularly generative metaphier, creating previously unspeakable distinctions in a throng of areas. The *head* of an army, table, page, bed, ship, household, or nail, or of steam or water; the *face* of a clock, cliff, card, or crystal; the *eyes* of needles, winds, storms, targets, flowers, or potatoes; the *brow* of a hill; the *cheeks* of a vise; the *teeth* of cogs or combs; the *lips* of pitchers, craters, augers; the *tongues* of shoes, boardjoints, or railway switches; the *arm* of a chair or the sea; the *leg* of a table, compass, sailor's voyage, or cricket field; and so on and on. Or the foot *of* this page. Or the *leaf* you will soon turn. All of these concrete metaphors increase enormously our powers of perception of the world about us and our understanding of it, and literally create new objects. Indeed, language is an organ of perception, not simply a means of communication. [. . .]

It is not always obvious that metaphor has played this all-important function. But this is because the concrete metaphors become hidden in phonemic change, leaving the words to exist on their own. Even such an unmetaphorical-sounding word as the verb 'to be' was generated from a metaphor. It comes from the Sanskrit *bhu*, 'to grow, or make grow,' while the English forms 'am' and 'is' have evolved from the same root as the Sanskrit *asmi*, 'to breathe.' It is something of a lovely surprise that the irregular conjugation of our most nondescript verb is thus a record of a time when man had no independent word for 'existence' and could only say that something 'grows' or that it 'breathes.'

Discussion

Glance back and check how many times I and the poets I cite use images to explain one or another point. Notice how many of those metaphors or similes are drawn from ordinary life – for the simple reason that images surround us. Ah, you may reply, but that's only the case for poets who have trained themselves to think in this way. Not if Jaynes is right.

I was sitting by the local pool thinking about this chapter while my daughter attended a swimming class, when I suddenly realised that the swimming instructor was talking in images. First she divided the class into seals and dolphins, and got each unit to swim like those creatures. Then she said, 'Imagine there's a ladder ahead of you in the water. Now stretch out your hands and grab this ladder and pull yourself through the gap.' First she used simile (saying they were *like* those creatures), then she used metaphor (pretending the water *was* a ladder they could grip). And, because imagery is an easy and natural way of learning, all the children did exactly what she asked. For them imagery was something to be experienced at a bodily level. Similarly, a good image in a poem induces something more than a superficial recognition; it resonates through the consciousness.

On the drive home we saw a large seagull stride across the pavement as though it were going to cross the road, only to stop as we passed. My daughter laughed, and said it looked like one of those businessmen with briefcases and squinty eyes. I tell you this not to bore you with how wonderful my daughter is (that might be a regrettable side effect), but in order to demonstrate how 'normal' imagery is. It's primarily a question of attention.

Activity 4.2   Reading and writing

Read 'Ode to Salt' by Pablo Neruda, from *Elemental Odes* (1991, pp. 366–9). Consider the order in which the images are presented.

Ode to Salt
This salt
in the saltcellar
I once saw in the salt mines.
I know
you won't
believe me,
but
it sings,
salt sings, the skin
of the salt mines
sings
with a mouth smothered
by the earth.
I shivered in those
solitudes
when I heard
the voice
of
the salt
in the desert.
Near Antofagasta
the nitrous
pampa
resounds:
a
broken
voice,
a mournful
song.
In its caves
the salt moans, mountain
of buried light,
translucent cathedral,
crystal of the sea, oblivion
of the waves.
And then on every table
in the world,
salt,

we see your piquant
powder
sprinkling
vital light
upon
our food.
Preserver
of the ancient
holds of ships,
discoverer
on
the high seas,
earliest
sailor
of the unknown, shifting
byways of the foam.
Dust of the sea, in you
the tongue receives a kiss
from ocean night:
taste imparts to every seasoned
dish your ocean essence;
the smallest,
miniature
wave from the saltcellar
reveals to us
more than domestic whiteness;
in it, we taste infinitude.

Now select an ordinary household object or substance, place it before you if it's moveable or place yourself before it if it's not. Write about it for 15 minutes focusing on attempting to produce as many images for it as possible.

Remember that although visual imagery may be your starting point, you have four other senses to consider – once you feel you've exhausted all the things it looks like, try finding images for its smell or feel. Don't go on to taste if it's a bottle of bleach or a carpet, but consider doing so if it's a slice of pizza or chocolate.

Discussion

This exercise explores the assertion that poetry can be made from ordinary things, indeed from almost anything. As Natalie Goldberg says:

> Learn to write about the ordinary. Give homage to old coffee cups, sparrows, city buses, thin ham sandwiches. Make a list of everything ordinary you can think of. Keep adding to it. Promise yourself, before you leave the earth, to mention everything on your list at least once in a poem, short story, newspaper article.
>
> (Goldberg 1986: 100)

Neruda's vision gradually transforms the 'normal' world. By the time he asserts that salt is 'Dust of the sea' you may even find yourself looking on dust in a new way: it's not quite 'salt of the land', but it is a kind of sandy beach forming in all our houses.

Are there any images you've produced that have this kind of transformative feel, making you think 'I could develop this'? If so, are they near the beginning or the end? The order you wrote your images in is at present random; it's a list rather than an argument. But that can be changed.

Look at the way Neruda's images are ordered: saltcellar, salt mine, voice of salt, cathedral, then a prefiguring of the sea image: 'crystal of the sea', then it returns to the domestic scene to start again: powder, light, preserver, sailor, then the second crescendo: 'Dust of the sea'. Each of these patterns seems fairly associative, but the order allows the poem to build and recede and build again to a climactic image, from which it subsides to the expansive gesture of the last line: 'in it, we taste infinitude.'

Spend 10 minutes on the order of your images. Are there any that run together? Are there some that stick out too much? Do they work standing by themselves? If so, where should they go? See if you can find an order that gives your list of images some rhetorical flow.

Poetry is, in essence, a natural response to being in the world, and having a language with which to express your reactions. The image is one of the means by which we respond to experience – everyone produces images, and indeed anyone could produce poems, but not everyone does, because it involves practice and effort to be good at it. A good poem is a formalised, almost ritual exchange between word and world, and the unit of currency is the image.

Received phrases

As I've said, one of the hardest things a writer learns to do is actually to read their own work. From first draft to proofing, we tend to see what we intend to write, rather than what appears on the page. A clear signal that this is happening is the appearance of received phrases, what people dismissively call clichés. Many received phrases are in fact tired images, and many mixed metaphors appear simply because the writer has over-looked the way that two phrases have metaphoric content and so clash with each other.

Attention to and elimination of the received phrase rejuvenates our writing at a basic level. Having to rethink the supposedly self-evident is not only good discipline; it ensures that we are concentrating on the fibre of our language. Paradoxically, many received phrases contain powerful images, but these have become worn away and invisible to us through overuse. Rethinking and rephrasing such expressions can lend our work a vernacular strength that an entirely new image sometimes lacks.

Activity 4.3   Reading

Read 'A Nutshell' by Simon Armitage, from *The Universal Home Doctor* (2002: 50–51). Can you identify the received phrases and proverbs this poem is using?

> **A Nutshell**
> It's too easy to mouth off, say
> how this matchwood and cotton ship of the line
> got where it is today.
>
> how it put into port,
> shouldered home through the narrow neck
> of a seamless, polished-off ten-year-old malt,
>
> came to be docked
> in a fish-eye, bell-jar, wide-angle bottle,
> shipshape and Bristol fashion.
>
> See, the whole thing was rigged,
> and righted itself at the tug of a string
> or turn of a screw, main mast raised

to its full height,
every detail correctly gauged, taffrail
to figurehead, a model of form

and scale, right down
to the glow of coal, and the captain,
toasting himself in the great cabin.

It's the same kind of loose talk
that cost us dear, put fire in the chimney breast,
smoking the stork from its nest.

At the end of the day, couldn't we meet
half-way, in an autumn field,
in the stubble of hay,

hearing the chink, chink, chink
of cheers, prost, mud in your eye, and stumble
through gate or arch,

to emerge on an apple orchard
in full cry, where tree after tree bends double
with glass, where every growth

blows a bubble or flask of fruit-in-the-bottle –
Jupiter, James Grieve, Ashmeads Kernel –
branch after branch of bottled fruit,

there for the picking, preserved in light?

Discussion

From the implied 'In' that could precede the title, this poem abounds with what we might think of as clichés, but, because the tone has a strange air of desperation to it, we may feel inclined to stick with it to its surreal conclusion. What do you think it's an image for, this orchard of bottled fruit? And what light does it cast back on the act of revealing how a ship gets into a bottle – a kind of visual cliché? The thickest grouping of familiar phrases occurs around a point of possible revelation:

It's the same kind of loose talk
that cost us dear, put fire in the chimney breast,
smoking the stork from its nest.

Here we glimpse that the subject of the poem may well be to do with fertility, or rather infertility. The stork which has been chased away makes us think again about the test-tube quality of those bottles of fruit. If this reading is right, then the poem is using its familiar phrases in a sharply ironic way: becoming pregnant as a commonplace event is described in language filled with commonplace expressions and images – except that being unable to conceive draws poignancy from those same expressions and images.

Activity 4.4   Writing

Make a list of the proverbial expressions commonly used in your family – the phrases that appear overused to you. When I did this, they turned out to be rather unusual expressions: 'canna see green cheese but her een birl' (can't see mouldy cheese without her eyes rolling) was said of a jealous person; 'auld age disna come itsel' (old age doesn't come itself) accompanied my grandmother's every arthritic pang; 'Eh well' was the stock response whenever someone was challenged and saw no reason either to engage with the challenge or back down.

Spend 15 minutes in the attempt to rehabilitate these phrases. One tactic suggested by Matthew Sweeney and John Hartley Williams in their book *Writing Poetry* is to take these phrases literally (1997: 32–4): what happened to her eyes when the woman saw the green cheese and how did the cheese get green in the first place? What and who accompanies old age and where have they all just arrived at? What might we find down an 'Eh' well?

Another strategy, following Armitage, is to imagine a situation in which such phrases could reacquire their original force. This could mean writing in persona, or constructing a scenario in which the cliché is the only possible concluding line.

There is in a sense no such thing as a cliché, only inattention to language and clichéd thinking. That's why I prefer the term 'received phrase', implying that you've used something given to you by someone else without doing enough work on it to make it your own. With care, any expression can find its role in your writing. With attention, the received phrase need never appear, you'll be so busy conjuring your own.

Attentiveness

Powerful imagery is based in powerful observation, in the ability to perceive intensely and originally. It connects us with the world about us in an intimate and enlivening manner. It is above all an act of engagement. The poet attempts to bind phenomena together through his or her senses, to perform acts of linkage that enable readers to experience their environment in different ways.

Learning to work with images involves training the eye, the ear, touch and taste and scent, to apprehend and define particulars. From the search for precise language arise equivalents to those particulars, so we must try to catch fugitive impressions and the comparisons that can come from them. By cultivating a vocabulary of images, we begin to cultivate the faculty of image-making.

In your daily practice this means working with your notebook in the way an artist works with a sketchbook. Carry it with you everywhere, and always give yourself permission to stop what you are doing, whenever possible, to make a note in it.

Whenever you see something that intrigues you – and it can be an interaction between two people at a zebra crossing or a plastic bag blown against a wire fence – describe it, and say what it is like. Start to think in images.

The important thing is not to prejudge what you're noting down. Don't decide beforehand that it's too trivial or irrelevant to your aims as a writer – you may find your aims have to adjust to meet some apparently random comment. Regularly comment on or rewrite these entries.

Activity 4.5   Reading

Read 'Summer Farm' by Norman MacCaig (2000: 435–6). How many images does he employ?

> **Summer Farm**
> Straws like tame lightnings lie about the grass
> And hang zigzag on hedges. Green as glass

The water in the horse-trough shines.
Nine ducks go wobbling by in two straight lines.

A hen stares at nothing with one eye,
Then picks it up. Out of an empty sky
A swallow falls and flickering through
The barn, dives up again into the dizzy blue.

I lie, not thinking, in the cool, soft grass,
Afraid of where a thought might take me – as
This grasshopper with plated face
Unfolds his legs and finds himself in space.

Self under self, a pile of selves I stand
Threaded on time, and with metaphysic hand
Lift the farm like a lid and see
Farm within farm, and in the centre, me.

Discussion

MacCaig began writing under the influence of Dylan Thomas and the 1940s writers known as Apocalyptics. His acute image-making faculty preserved something of that period's surrealist power. Objects are seen with an intensity that's leavened by a deadpan wit: what on earth are 'tame lightnings'? What a great deal of energy to give to a piece of straw.

'A hen looks at nothing with one eye/then picks it up' is at first reading a witty line. Then we consider the implications of the speaker being 'afraid of where a thought might take [him]', and the picture gains an emotional intensity. That 'nothing' which the hen pecks at has more than a whiff of the void; and the alarming ease with which the grasshopper finds itself 'in space' prepares for the existential image in the last stanza.

MacCaig's imagery is not just for show. It helps to build the message of the poem, and it underscores its tone. It is doing imaginatively what the poem is saying, making us experience what, otherwise, might be a purely intellectual proposition. Some amateur poets just leave us with the thought, and fail to engage us on the level of the image. And plenty of professionals dazzle with imagery, but forget to align this to the message of the poem. You must learn to do both.

Activity 4.6   Writing

For a period of not less than 24 hours, keep your notebook to hand, open and ready to jot things down in. On the kitchen table, in the office, in the shopping trolley – on the bedside table beside you when you're asleep. Write things down whenever they occur to you – with one proviso: only write down images. The top of my boiled egg sits on my plate like half a meteor. The paperclips lie on top of each other like sleeping ants. The uncooked chicken looks like a smacked bottom. My partner is snoring like an exhausted lumberjack.

For 24 hours, think in images, packs of them like timber wolves in a shopping mall. Give yourself over to a way of looking at the world, like an optician in a bath full of spectacles. And note them all down, like a special constable arresting a parrot.

Discussion

Becoming good at imagery is primarily a matter of perfecting the technique of transmission: how efficiently you get your impressions down on paper. You must first become alert to the possibility of image-making, then give yourself space to pursue that possibility, and finally become adept at recording it precisely. Think of the difference between the amateur and professional photographer: one takes pictures only of those things they want to remember; the other photographs what they want everyone to remember. One takes a few pictures, the other shoots off reel after reel.

Formulae of imagery

A mixed metaphor is merely the incorrect form of a highly useful tool. More considered combinations of images can create interesting atmospheres and even rhetorical effects. Just as a single image gives tone, a succession of images can build up layers of resonance. A coherent progression of images has an almost argumentative force, and some poets construct poems almost as a formula of images which adds up to produce a specific effect in the reader. This is for many readers a glimpse of the further levels of meaning which poetry can manipulate.

For instance, look back at Chapter 3 on Voice. In Activity 3.2 I suggested you wrote an acrostic based on your first name, then in the subsequent paragraphs I gave four sample words: 'bowling' 'ikebana' 'licentious' and

'Luddite'. These are, of course, an acrostic of my name. My point is: while doing one thing, poetic language is usually doing another, and a chain of images is one means by which this is accomplished.

Glance back at that remark I made in Activity 4.2 in response to Neruda's line, claiming that dust was a beach in our homes. That reaction, inverting Neruda's image and checking it for sense, illustrates something peculiar to poetry. In a poem, metaphor is very much a method of thought. At the first level it's how observation is integrated with reflection: I see A, hmm, that reminds me of B. At the second level it's a method of generating ideas: if A is like B, then I can talk about A in the way I usually talk about B.

So, if dust is like the sand you find on a beach, then I can talk about my study or windowsill or mantelpiece, as though it is a beach. As Jaynes suggests, language is often there before us when it comes to metaphor: my bookshelf is echoed by the shelf of land that extends into the waves, off which I could dive into a sea of associations. But why?

One reason is certainly to be witty, showing yourself off to the reader as able to think nimbly in a pattern. Another more interesting reason is to allow the pattern to help you think, to use a chain of images to take you somewhere you might not have got to without them. And this touches on an important aspect of writing poetry.

Poetry as an art form invites us to go beyond our preconceptions, to invent, to be truly imaginative. One reason for this is because that action, of going beyond ourselves, is an effect of the form itself: the poem is a structure which helps us to think differently, and one of the ways it does this is through its focus on imagery, encouraging us to think through our images in rational or irrational patterns.

Activity 4.7   Reading

Read 'A Free Translation' by Craig Raine, from *Rich* (1984: 36–8). Again, look at the images, but this time consider the connections between them.

A Free Translation
for Norma Kitson

Seeing the pagoda
of dirty dinner plates,
I observe my hands

under the kitchen tap
as if they belonged
to Marco Polo:

glib with soap,
they speak of details
from a pillow book,

the fifty-seven ways
in which the Yin
receives the Yang.

Rinsed and purified,
they flick off drops
like a court magician

whose stretching fingers
seek to hypnotize
the helpless house . . .

This single bullrush
is the silent firework
I have invented

to amuse the children.
Slow sideboard sparkler,
we watch its wadding

softly fray.
Your skein of wool
sleeps on the sofa,

a geisha girl
with skewered hair,
too tired to think

of loosening ends,
or fret forever
for her Samurai,

whose shrunken ghost
attacks the window pane –
still waspish

in his crisp corselet
of black and gold
hammered out by Domaru.

In coolie hats,
the peasant dustbins
hoard their scraps,

careless of the warrior class . . .
It is late, late:
we have squeezed

a fluent ideogram
of cleansing cream
across the baby's bottom.

It is time to eat
the rack of pork
which curves and sizzles

like a permanent wave
by Hokusai,
time to bend

to a bowl of rice,
time to watch
your eyes become

Chinese with laughter
when I say that
orientals eat with stilts.

Discussion

This is an instance of a Martian poem. Martianism was a short-lived literary phenomenon of the 1980s, in which clever use of metaphor was the dominant characteristic. It sometimes seemed clever for its own sake, but occasionally you felt the purpose of the re-visioning was to make you think differently.

Here Raine imposes an overarching conceit: everything in this kitchen and this house has an oriental aspect. (Note that this is also reflected at a structural level: the poem is in three-line, haiku-like stanzas.) The integration of the imagery serves a purpose, allowing the meditative exactitude of Chinese and Japanese poetry to reshape this very English scene.

Activity 4.8   Writing

Consider your list of images for objects from Activity 4.6, and the list of images for the household object you produced in Activity 4.2. Take one image from each that you think shows promise. Now apply that image to the other object. For instance, if you said that the paperclips in your office were like sleeping ants, and that a slice of pizza was like a town being covered in lava, now try those images out the other way round. In what sense is your office desk like a town beneath a volcano? What does a slice of pizza have to do with ants?

Well, the computer is continually emitting emails and printouts: could they be like lava? Are the paperclips now the trapped population of Pompeii? As for that pizza, capers could well be ant heads and olives ant bodies, anchovies could be worms and Parma ham the wings of butterflies. Ew!

Write for 10 minutes on each possibility.

The effort of getting an image that 'should' apply to one thing to fit onto something quite different obliges us to think clearly about the rules of the image, those elements which enabled us to map it onto the object in the first place. A was like B because elements of A corresponded to elements of B; if C is also to be like B, then we must define those elements of B clearly enough to look for them in C.

One effect of this exercise it that it can produce unexpected and disturbing chains of imagery (insect pizza indeed!), which brings us on to my next point. Images don't have to make sense.

The image is also a profound source of irrational power within a poem. Instead of making a piece cohere, it can also be a way of disrupting habits of thought or casual assumptions. To return to the metaphor of the formula, sometimes the links between images aren't plus signs but minuses, and not every poem should reach a definite controlled conclusion. Through imagery we can glimpse the unconscious motives which drive us, and we must learn when to trust an unusual, mysterious or even destabilising image.

Activity 4.9   Reading and writing

Read Selima Hill's 'Portrait of my Lover as a Strange Animal', from *Portrait of my Lover as a Horse* (2002: 67). How do these images make you feel?

Portrait of My Lover as a Strange Animal
Don't ask me why
but soon I started feeding it,
on caterpillars, chocolate drops, soft fruit –
anything as long as it was small.
Its mouth was as small and tight as a wedding-ring.
On moonlit nights it liked to watch the stars
and lean against me
like a giant jelly.
Then came the night I thought I heard it speak.
It said my name!
O Lord, it sounded beautiful! . . .
But of course by then I was out of my mind with exhaustion.
I had sunk to my knees in the sand I was so exhausted.
And the sacks I had carried contained only roots.
And as for my name –
it was only the sound of its gums
crunching the body
of its final wren.

As the title of Selima Hill's collection suggests, this entire book is taken up with a series of portraits, very few of which can be said to be based on a visual stimulus. These images arise from a powerful concretising imagination, which can take quite abstract ideas and qualities, and find a way of embodying them.

Some of these images clearly refer to elements of a relationship: 'Its mouth was as small and tight as a wedding-ring.' Others are finding form for more amorphous, disturbing aspects of intimacy: the depersonalised 'it' of the lover leans against her 'like a giant jelly'. Still others seem inexplicable, but nonetheless carry a strong emotive charge, and Hill, significantly, chooses to end with the most unsettling of these:

> . . . the sound of its gums
> crunching the body
> of its final wren.

Think back to the exercise I set you in Activity 3.2 in the chapter about voice: you had to come up with a series of words you liked, half of which could be words you liked because of their sense. That's an abstract way of approaching language, so were any of these actual abstractions, such as beauty or horror, boredom or heartiness, bemusement or honesty? Either pick one from your list or select a new abstraction that you now feel sums up something of your interests as a writer. What quality or value might you be exploring recurrently in your work?

Now write for 15 minutes, concentrating on embodying this abstraction in a series of images in the following manner:

- Imagine the abstraction is in a box, and this box has a circular hole in the top, just big enough for your hand. Put your hand into the box and touch the abstraction: what does it feel like?
- Now put your nose to the hole and sniff: what precisely does it smell like?
- Listen to the abstraction: what does it sound like? Is it saying anything?
- Imagine putting your mouth to the hole and tentatively sticking out your tongue: what does it taste like?
- Now take the abstraction out of the box and hold it in your arms: is this even possible? What is it like to hold? Does it have feelings? Can you tell how it feels about you?
- Drop it: what does it do?

Discussion

Sometimes images can seem contradictory and even inexplicable. Our task is to gauge the kind of energy they contain, and decide whether it's right for a particular poem. Sometimes this energy is so strong that it demands a poem of its own, or, in Hill's case, generates an entire book. Sometimes you have to trust what you don't quite understand. T.S. Eliot famously remarked that to appreciate a poem it wasn't necessary at first to understand it. The finest poetry yields up new meanings every time we read it.

A lot of people are put off poetry because they can't tolerate the fact they don't fully understand something the first time they read it. They read nuance as nuisance, complexity as confusion. Lovers of poetry learn patience because they know that the payback is usually far richer than any instant hit. Poetry is an attempt to find words for sensations, states of mind or perceptions which previously seemed to lack words – this is what Pope meant when he said 'True wit' consisted of 'What oft was thought but ne'er so well expressed'. What helps people to tolerate the delay in gratification is often the music of the language, which is why we shall go on next to look at rhyme.

The image is one of the basic building blocks of poetry, like line and rhyme. It is important because, like those devices, it focuses our attention on language and what language does. At a primary level, language conjures images: I say 'dog' to an English speaker, and they imagine some type of dog; I say 'chien' and they imagine some kind of poodle. Not only do they imagine the animal, they have an immediate, uncontrolled reaction to it: dog-lovers see an Irish setter streaming across a field; dogophobes see a pit bull squeezing out something disgusting on a blasted pavement. The image, then, is your remote control to the reader's brain – they're usually in charge of this, but for the short time they consent to read a poem, you've got it. Press the buttons wisely.

References

Armitage, Simon (2002) *The Universal Home Doctor*. London: Faber and Faber.

Goldberg, Natalie (1986) *Writing Down the Bones: Freeing the writer within*. Boston: Shambhala.

Hill, Selima (2002) 'Portrait of My Lover as a Strange Animal', in *Portrait of my Lover as a Horse*. Tarset: Bloodaxe Books.

MacCaig, Norman (2000) 'Summer Farm', in Robert Crawford and Mick Imlah (eds) *The New Penguin Book of Scottish Verse*. London: Penguin.

Neruda, Pablo (1991) 'Ode to Salt', in *Elemental Odes*, Margaret Sayers Peden (tr.). London: Libris.

Raine, Craig (1984) 'A Free Translation', in *Rich*. London: Faber and Faber.

Sweeney, Matthew and Williams, John Hartley (1997) *Writing Poetry: and getting published*. London: Hodder Headline.

Part 2

Dialogue: Linda France (LF) and Bill Herbert (BH)

BH: It often seems to me that imagery is an entry point to poetry for people because the image is such an ordinary part of language and the way that people see the world. Do you think that imagery is something natural or something very particular to the way that a poet thinks?

LF: I think it is natural. You notice it in the way that children speak about things. As soon as language comes, image comes, it seems to me. I think it's connected to Blake's Doors of Perception, how we perceive the world as a human being and we do that through our five senses. So even though you are speaking about images, which we normally think of as visual, I think that they are connected with all the five senses, and probably other ones that we can't even pin down into that particular format. So as long as you're existing in the world and you are awake, really, then you're going to notice that you're sitting on a chair and it feels soft or hard, pleasant or unpleasant; or you'll notice, as soon as you are aware of the breath coming in that that will be happening in a certain way – if you are indoors or outdoors, what the temperature is like, how you're feeling. So that I think moves into the sixth sense. You've got these different perceptions to do with how something feels, smells, touches, tastes, appears before our eyes and then, immediately, that triggers, a response in us, our particular response at that time.

BH: So why do we reach for analogies? Is it to communicate to others what it feels like, to be sitting in a place, to be breathing in a way, or is there another reason for using an image?

LF: Well I think mostly, and certainly for myself, it's to make sense of it. I think that's one of the things that poetry does, Robert Frost's idea of it as a momentary stay against confusion.

BH: When you are reaching for imagery, does what you produce tend to be visual, tactile? What's your experience of creating imagery?

LF: I think when I first started writing it used to be more the visual that came first, and I've often thought that I was a poet because I couldn't be an artist. But actually, in terms of how my work's developed, I've become more interested in the physical and the tactile. The visual often only presents the surface of things, and I'm actually interested in going below that, to how something is experienced almost from the inside, the armature, if you like. There's something about writing from the body, as we speak about it, that allows one to do that, so I've become more and more interested in that.

BH: That's looking at imagery as a way of describing the tangible world around us and, of course, the other thing that it is, is the way of describing the world within us, of making concrete that which is not.

LF: Yes, and I guess the ideal is bringing the two together: you want the two to come together so it doesn't become disembodied – neither disembodied nor so thoroughly rooted that it stays almost inert or fossilised or stagnant; so there's some kind of dynamic that occurs. That's what the image seems to me to be offering the potential of, that transformation. The very word 'metaphor' suggests transformation, so you are turning something from your perception into something else in the act of writing about it.

BH: So it's a way of renewing, not just your work, not just your writing, but renewing yourself?

LF: Yes, I don't think you can separate the two, really. I can't separate the two. Yes, but also on a simpler level, transformation in the sense of change, really; that there's this sense of change and exchange. There's yourself in relation to the world and your experience, and it's what you perceive and, in writing about it, in articulating it, you are giving it back to the world as well, so, again, that kind of dynamic is constantly happening.

BH: How do people go about developing their imagery, their sense of the world through images?

LF: It seems to me it comes back to that idea of being awake, just being aware of yourself and your connection with the world. So that's the other thing a metaphor does, and simile as well, it expresses the interconnectedness of all things. It's saying that this thing is like something else or this thing is something else. So, there is a possible arbitrariness that you could say about what the eye alights upon and life's a bit like, it's just very accidental, the way we move around the world. And so what we happen to bump into, what we happen to read or whatever picture we see in a gallery that we choose to become particularly fascinated in, there's a sort of serendipitous side to it, but it's almost whatever happens to stay with us, and the connections that we make.

BH: There's almost a playfulness to what you were saying there. In art (and you talked about painting and drawing earlier), the artist is always able to sketch. Is there a similar thing that the writer does that's sketching but is also developing this ability to see, this ability to respond? Can they, for instance, decide they are going to compare everything today to a sheep and then go round looking for sheepiness in lots of things?

LF: Yes, I guess. I know that I do that with extended metaphor in a poem, where you get snagged by a particular connection that you've made between one thing and another which isn't that thing but they go together quite nicely and produce an interesting spark. If it's sufficiently interesting, and you stick with it and follow it through, then it might result in a whole poem that's just playing around that one central idea. I've done it with food, I've done it with language, I've done it with certain animals: anything that's generic, really, seems to offer the potential for that kind of interpretation. This poem came from a commission: I had to write to a line which was 'I woke up with dried blood under my fingernails,' which filled me with horror, but as soon as I decided – and I don't know where the idea's from – but as soon as I decided that it was going to be about food, I actually got the copy of Delia Smith's cookery book off my shelf and read through the index at the back, and just all that list of the titles of recipes and foods, it was like eating a very large rich meal.

Cooking with Blood
Last night I dreamt of Delia Smith again –
smoked buckling simmering on the horizon,
that old Doverhouse moon stuffing the dumpling
of a crackling sky. She played en papillote

for just long enough to sweat me garlicky.
After I'd peppered her liver, stuffed her goose
and dogfished her tender loins, she was paté
in my hands. She got all mulligatawny

so I tossed her into a nine herb salad
of Hintlesham. She was my Russian herring,
my giblet stock. We danced the ossobuco;
her belly kedgeree, her breasts prosciutto.

I tongue-casseroled her ear she was my Queen
of Puddings and wouldn't we sausage lots
of little quichelets, a platter of sprats
we'd name Béarnaise, Mortadella, Bara brith.

But when the trout hit the Tabasco, it turned out
she was only pissaladière, garam
masala as a savoyard. Arrowroot.
Just another dip in love with crudités.

And I've stroganoffed with too many of them.
I chopped home to my own bloater paste and triped
myself into a carcass. No wonder I woke up
with scarlet farts, dried blood under my fingernails,

dreaming of Delia, her oxtail, again.

BH: So it's not just finding one metaphor. It's also the ability to conjure and extend, almost creating like a formula of how the metaphors relate to each other across a poem, how the imagery adds up. Is that a way that you work in frequently?

LF: I think of it as creating a world, really. One of the things that you do as a writer is have the opportunity to play God: you are able to create a world that has its own integrity, has its own laws, has its own climate, has its own culture, and, and that might be what happens when you are able to go to this place where there's this exploration of a particular theme, idea, area of language, whatever it might be.

BH: So the metaphor almost forms a kind of language in itself, so that the language of a poem can be doing one thing but the metaphor in the poem can be doing something further that augments it or even contradicts it?

LF: Well, yes, it does that. I've never thought of it that way but it is like you're translating something into almost a new language of your own invention. It does feel a little bit like, in attempting to create that, you have to be prepared to stumble, it seems to me. Getting the register right, so that the world is coherent in the poem, it's almost inevitable that you fall off now and then and I quite like those falling off places because it shows that it's not real, that it is a game, in some sense.

BH: But not all metaphor works as a pattern or a game, sometimes imagery comes from a disturbing zone, or a place that we don't necessarily fully understand when we come up with it. We don't quite know where it comes from. How do you find those things, and then how do you deal with them once you've found them?

LF: In 2001 a friend of mine, another poet called Andrew Waterhouse, committed suicide and I wrote this poem for him.

Trying to Explain Telescope
Telescope. A device for looking
at the world from a distance.
If you were from the moon
I'd just been watching through one,
the magnificent, unfathomable mirror
of its lens – open mouthed at curves,
halo, pockmarks, its surface pitted
as pumice and close as my own heels –
if that was where you came from,
where we must assume there are no
telescopes, I'd show you one. Here:
the shiny black cylinder, hard
and scientific; the way it collapses
into itself, becoming smaller, blind
and of no use. I'd demonstrate how
you can lift it, open, to your eye
and look at the stars, their late blaze,
their conjuring of swan and horse
and fog. You would discover more
shapes, other functions. We might share
what we both know is cracked laughter.
How can I not let you keep it
in your hands, a gift to mark
our meeting, our almost total
lack of comprehension.

LF: In the days immediately after I heard about his death, I was very distressed and disturbed by hearing the news and, as often happens with grief, it didn't make any sense, particularly in this instance because of the manner of his death. And one of the things that kept happening, as well as the re-running of memories of times we shared together, I just seemed to get this recurring image almost behind my eyes of a telescope or of what appeared to be a telescope, a long black cylindrical object and the nearest I could get to what it must possibly be was a telescope. That's the only thing that I could think of because it just kept coming so frequently and so insistently that I knew I had to . . . well, what is this, it's almost like a hallucination, it was quite disturbing. It seemed to me to say something about the way that he looked at the world, in his poetry in particular, but also in his life. I actually say 'a device for looking at the world from a distance', but it was also something that he might have written: a poem about looking at the world through a telescope. So it was a way of becoming nearer to him too, the way that you do when someone you care about is no longer there for you. So even though I really didn't know what was happening at all with this image, I decided to just risk it and write about it as if it were a telescope, and just go with it and do it with some sense of appreciation of him in mind, and it would take care of itself.

BH: People often read poems thinking 'What's it about, what's the message?' as though there was something that could be extracted from the experience of reading the poem that will give them it in a nutshell, but the process you are describing is really quite different: it's about living with something and tolerating not immediately getting it, allowing those other layers to come through gradually. I'm curious how is it that we learn to tolerate not understanding: is there something the poem does that compensates us for this, or is there some way this slow release is made palatable to us?

LF: Yes, I think that a poem is a thing of pleasure; a poem is something that brings pleasure and a lot of that comes from the language – again the love of language – so the joy that you get from an elegant use of words, the sound, the images that come in our minds and the way that we're changed by it. We might not know why or how but we are changed by it. The act of change that the writer has had to experience to create it, in their sharing of that, we are able to experience a similar process in reading it.

BH: So the image, the idea of the metaphor as something changing into something else, is really quite key to the whole poetic experience for you? Not only is it recording how the writer changes from one thing into another thing, but it's also recording how the reader changes, as a result of that experience, as a result of reading that. So metaphor is really a central part of that whole process: is that how important it is for you in your work?

LF: Yes. But I might not necessarily think of that. If you start making connections between things that appear to be disparate then they start happening all on their own. You do see the connections between things that aren't simply of your own making, and other people see them too, I believe. I do think that we live in a world that is connected. It might appear chaotic but it has its own kind of coherence and elegance as well, so the connections are there to be made.

BH: One issue which arises from this, which I think is quite important for poets, is how much they know about why they are doing something: with an image, once you've uncovered all the secrets as it were, you've almost killed it off. Is there a sense in which the writer has to be in a state of unknowing? Does that mean that you are constantly developing because as soon as you learn something you have to do it differently?

LF: Er, at the risk of sounding terribly dilettante, I think that might well be the case, yes. There's a sense of the hook that in the metaphor, in particular, works like that, that you're always in pursuit. I always, often feel in pursuit of something which I'm destined never to be able to actually grasp so it's like I'm always wanting to write the poem that I'm never going to be able to write, that will just cap it all – it will save me from having to write any other poem, and it's almost like I will find the metaphor for that . . . Having said that, I also find myself returning to images again and again so I might feel as if I've done something to death like, I mentioned before, food or language or animals. And then I'll go so far with it but I'll find it coming up again years later, and needing to go back there and revisit it – that idea that we're only really writing the same poem over and over anyway. If the poem as poem is simply an image, a metaphor for something else, a mirror of our subconscious or our perception of the world, whatever it may be, then it's almost inevitable that, even though we are changing, we still have the same doors usually, so through those doors the same things will parade and keep on coming.

BH: So metaphor, in that sense, can almost be a way of exploring theme; you return to certain themes through looking at how you've used metaphor, through looking at the metaphors that worked most powerfully for you.

LF: I think so. Yeah, that's how it worked for me. So I think metaphor, the way we normally speak about metaphor as a figure of speech, saying something is something else, rather than simile which is saying something is like something else, so it actually becomes it, that's the transformation that occurs. But it's not simply that, I think that it is in becoming something else, it becomes much, much bigger, and moves into the area of what we normally think of as symbol, that whole area of symbolic language, something representing something else, standing for something else over the scale of a whole poem, rather than just three or four lines within a poem. The more poems I write I find that happening more and more, that things are rarely what they seem anyway, that it's just as easy to speak about them as being something else, and when it's something else or when something does occur, it always seems to me to offer the potential for it to be speaking about something else. So everything is something else, or everything has the potential to be something else and I love that, it's like some Chinese box or Russian doll or Hall of Mirrors . . .

BH: You're even using images to describe this process.

LF: Yes, because it's endless, actually, it is endless, it seems to me.

BH: But this is not just random transference of things: you are looking to discover something about the original object by enacting this transformation, aren't you?

LF: Yes. You are. You're almost wanting to make the thing, the object or the experience or whatever it is that you are perceiving, or wanting to write about, you are wanting to make an image in the reader's mind that will almost be truer than the thing itself. It's a little bit like the medieval idea of the law of correspondences: as above, so it is below. Everything that happens on this universal, astronomical, astrological, alchemical level, has its own counterpoint in an actual world, so flowers and herbs in particular but also minerals. So if we reduced the universe to elements, that's all we are anyway. We are only those elements ourselves, so we will see those elements in everything around us.

BH: This is a very serious form of playfulness then, or it's a very playful form of seriousness. You talked about symbols earlier. We think about symbols like the cross or the rose, and these are things which are seen as slightly beyond ordinary experience and beyond our ordinary powers to invent but the world you are talking about and inventing seems much more accessible, as something which we can all do. Do you think that this image-making faculty is within us all?

LF: Yes. I do. Religion does it very specifically, both through the language and the ritual, but we all create, human beings create ritual, whether they're taught it or they're encouraged to or not, simply in terms of their habits. And so we naturally create our own myths. Human beings want to invest some of themselves: we are very generous beings and so we want to invest some of ourselves. We are also greedy, aren't we, so we want to give something of ourselves to the thing and we want something back from it too. And that's where the communication side of it comes too: when we write something we want to share it and we want that sharing to be valid and helpful to people.

BH: So the metaphor almost becomes the unit of exchange?

LF: Yes, at that particular time we will come up with a certain connection, a certain correspondence, a certain metaphor, but the more particular we are, it seems to me, the more universal we will be. So the more we tell the truth about our actual physical experience of the world of that morning or that day or that terrible night, the more someone else will see their own experience mirrored in it. I'm going to read a poem called 'Body Language' and I have an epigraph from Milan Kundera's novel, *The Unbearable Lightness of Being*, where he says, 'Metaphors are dangerous. Metaphors are not to be trifled with. A single metaphor can give birth to love.'

> Before, she used to need a translator
> to understand what his body language
> signified, its present tense. She declined
> the metaphor of eye contact, explored
> the academic use of pseudonym.
>
> *Why is the alphabet in that order?'*
> was one of many unsettling questions
> provoked by the microfiche of letters,
> dinner, too much whiskey. Bed was always
> conditional; might be superlative.

When the VDU bleated *insert, text,*
merge, she couldn't process the words on the tip
of her tongue, nipple, hip, solar plexus,
clitoris: the cowardice of one who
knew what systole meant, diastole, oscillation.

References

France, Linda (2002) 'Cooking with Blood', in *The Simultaneous Dress*. Tarset: Bloodaxe Books, p. 46.

France, Linda (2002) 'Trying to Explain Telescope', in *The Simultaneous Dress*. Tarset: Bloodaxe Books, p. 60.

France, Linda (1994) 'Body Language', in *The Gentleness of the Very Tall*. Newcastle: Bloodaxe Books, p. 56.

5

Rhyme

Part 1

Poetry is always trying to achieve a perfect balance between sound and sense. It is as aware of the music of language as it is of its meaning. Rhyme involves an act of linkage, an awareness of pattern: it explores the associativeness of sound. As such it doesn't simply take place at the ends of lines, and it doesn't concern itself only with the full rhymes traditionally placed there.

Rhyme in its fullest sense is the attempt to integrate the sound of language with the particular shape, tone and sense of a poem. In order to do this rhyme must be free to occur throughout a poem in all its possible manifestations – as we'll see, assonance, consonance and slant rhyme are all part of the act of rhyming, as indeed is dissonance and the obtrusive patterns of comic rhyme.

You still occasionally hear the complaint during the questions that end poetry readings that modern poetry doesn't rhyme. I usually reply, 'Anglo-Saxon poetry and Middle English poetry doesn't rhyme either – and neither does most of Shakespeare and Milton and long stretches of Wordsworth. It's a disgrace!' What the complainer often means is that their impression of modern poetry doesn't rhyme, this impression being formed from a recollection of early modernism (around and after the First World War), and a partial awareness of the poetry of the 1960s and early 1970s. Of course, just as in the past, contemporary poetry doesn't have to rhyme, but, as Michael Longley tells us, that doesn't mean it doesn't want to:

> A lot of modern poetry, I insist, does rhyme. My own gifted contemporaries, Seamus Heaney and Derek Mahon, work with equal ease in free forms and in stricter conventional stanzas that use rhyme-schemes. A younger Ulster poet, Paul Muldoon, has taken the art of rhyme to new heights of subtlety and sophistication. A virtuoso deployment of rhyme has been a feature of Northern Irish poetry for more than three decades. Every line in my own first collection rhymes. I now rhyme only occasionally. Rhyme is one of the things that words do. In as much as poetry takes advantage of all those things, I regret not using rhyme more frequently (though receptive always to assonance, its clashes and chimes). When asked where he got his ideas from, Yeats sounded as though he was joking, but he was in fact hinting at a mystery: 'Looking for the next rhyme,' he replied. (Longley in Curtis 1996: 118)

'Rhyme is one of the things that words do' is a statement I'm particularly fond of. Not just because of the implied 'just' appearing between 'is' and 'one', but also because of the sheer matter-of-factness of it. Imagery is also one of the things words do; so is metre. Basically, so is poetry. Poets tend to get on with it; it's people who aren't writing poetry who fret most about these things. So let's write.

Activity 5.1   Reading

Look at the diagram below. This is what I (using the power of metaphor) call a 'Rhymewell'. I've dropped one of my keywords from Chapter 3, 'lascivious', into the centre. Then I've filled the nearer 'ripples' with fuller rhymes, and the farther out ones with less full rhymes.

As you can see, apart from 'oblivious', the only truly full rhymes for 'lascivious' are concentrated on the very last syllable – even these aren't exact, as the 's' sound is softer in 'lascivious' than in 'muss' (and the stress is stronger). As soon as we try to include two or more syllables in our rhyme, then the closest is 'devious' in which the vowel sound before the 'v' has changed slightly. If we abandon the 'v', more words come into play (including Lewis Carroll's nonsense word 'frumious'), but we're

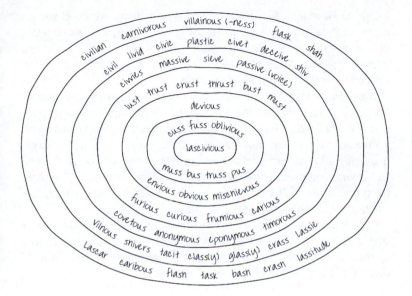

beginning to establish that English isn't a great language for unadulter-
ated full rhyme. ('Passive voice', however, is an interesting near rhyme –
remember that you don't have to match a single word to a single word
when rhyming.)

What English is very good at is sounds that shade into each other, and
those are the other words you'll find in this ripple. By adding the letter 't'
to my monosyllabic 'truss' and 'muss' rhymes, I find a pack of suggestive
terms highly appropriate to rhyme with 'lascivious': 'bust' 'thrust' and
'lust' don't seem to be in any doubt what they're about. By the time we
move out to the next ripple, I've flattened that 'ious' ending to include
rhymes like 'anonymous'. I've also extended my search to look for rhymes
on the stressed sound 'lasciv' – the reader's ear will still be able to pick
this up, so I can rhyme on 'sieve', and even (by shifting the stress a little)
on '**mass**ive'.

By the next few ripples there's a wide variety of possibilities, but some
of them are starting to sound a bit remote ('shivers' – can you still hear
that?) – I'm clearly approaching the rim of the well. There are still good
rhymes out here, though, and even some surprising ones: 'carnivorous' is
rhythmically a good match, and so 'obvious' I should have noticed it

earlier. My favourite, though, is 'caribous' – its first two vowel sounds rhyme with 'lasciv' (this is what we call assonantal rhyme), but its last is only an eye rhyme for 'ous' (an eye rhyme is something that looks like it should rhyme, but doesn't when you actually say it). There's something about 'lascivious caribous' I find endearing.

There are a lot of words in this well, all more or less related to each other. If I'd stuck with the notion of full rhyme, I might have got two or three ripples out, but I wouldn't necessarily have happened upon 'carnivorous' and may never have noticed 'sieve'. The well method generates a lot of terms to throw into the mix when you're drafting something, and it's more organic than a rhyming dictionary. The other thing it does, as you'll have noticed at the end of my last paragraph, is create associations.

I may never write a poem about a carnivorous villainness and a curious shah in Vilnous, with guest appearances by an anonymous Lascar and, of course, two massive plastic (and crassly lascivious) caribous, but if I don't, it obviously won't be for lack of rhymes.

Activity 5.2   Writing

Pick a word from your original list of favourites or look for one in a draft you're already working on. Drop it in the Rhymewell and start listening. Try to get beyond the first few ripples and keep your ear alert for surprising terms. Do this for 10 minutes.

When you find yourself bumping up against the brickwork at the edge of the well, take the last term, the one you're least sure rhymes but are quite pleased to discover (mine would be 'caribous'). Drop it in a new well and start again. Give this another 10 minutes.

Now play with terms from both Rhymewells. Form associative patterns and see where they take you. Don't worry too much about making sense, and incorporate any other rhymes that occur to you as you write. Give this yet another 10 minutes.

Rhyme is all about the liveliness of your ear. The more attention you pay to the sounds of words, the more supple and responsive your own word selection becomes. Techniques like the Rhymewell shift us out of familiar habits of listening and help us to look into the hearts of words. Sometimes the things we find there are magical.

Look again at that last line by Neruda, or rather, at that line by Neruda's translator, Margaret Sayers Peden: 'in it, we taste infinitude'. Look in the words in the way the Rhymewell looked in 'lascivious'. Ah yes, repetition, the fullest rhyme of all: '*in it*, we taste inf *in it* ude.' Now there's a line that does exactly what it says on the label.

Full

If imagery is principally poetry's reclamation of the eye from disengaged, casual observation, then rhyme is how the poem reclaims our ear. The perfect rhyme can sometimes seem to point beyond itself, to contain sense in itself, though all the time we know it's the result of a happy coincidence of sounds. It can lend weight to utterance and strongly underscore conclusions.

It can also trivialise an idea by making it sound too pat. Full rhymes can sometimes feel expected, and even encourage facile composition, where the sense is being strung between uninventive sounds. Sometimes we can fall into accidental patterns of full rhyme in the same way as we occasionally employ received phrases and don't notice.

In other words the considered use of full rhyme is a powerful tool, and learning when to deploy it is a discipline we must acquire.

Activity 5.3   Reading

Read 'Leaving Inishmore' by Michael Longley, from *Selected Poems* (1998: 22). What effect if any does the way the poem rhymes have on your reading?

> **Leaving Inishmore**
> Rain and sunlight and the boat between them
> Shifted whole hillsides through the afternoon –
> Quiet variations on an urgent theme
> Reminding me now that we left too soon
> The island awash in wave and anthem.
>
> Miles from the brimming enclave of the bay
> I hear again the Atlantic's voices,
> The gulls above us as we pulled away –
> So munificent their final noises
> These are the broadcasts from our holiday.

Oh, the crooked walkers on that tilting floor!
And the girls singing on the upper deck
Whose hair took the light like a downpour –
Interim nor change of scene shall shipwreck
Those folk on the move between shore and shore.

Summer and solstice as the seasons turn
Anchor our boat in a perfect standstill,
The harbour wall of Inishmore astern
Where the Atlantic waters overspill –
I shall name this the point of no return

Lest that excursion out of light and heat
Take on a January idiom –
Our ocean icebound when the year is hurt,
Wintertime past cure – the curriculum
Vitae of sailors and the sick at heart.

Discussion

This is a poem from Longley's first book, *No Continuing City*, in which, as he says in the passage quoted earlier in this chapter, every line rhymes. It marks a theme that recurs again and again in his poetry: the west of Ireland and its islands as a refuge, whether for his family, moral values, or the natural world, against traumas of all sorts – the First World War his father fought in, and the Troubles, which were to rock his subsequent work.

The poem focuses on the point of departure, so has an elegiac air, but performs a curious action: it freezes things at that point:

Summer and solstice as the seasons turn
Anchor our boat in a perfect standstill,
The harbour wall of Inishmore astern
Where the Atlantic waters overspill –
I shall name this the point of no return

The moment of solstice coincides with the moment of departure, and Longley poises the poem here, after departure but before arrival, since arrival involves change, threat, decay – note all those terms from illness in the last stanza: 'the year is hurt,/Wintertime past cure . . . the sick at heart.'

Exploiting the way that a poem records a single event by emphasising that the poem will preserve that moment forever is an old literary trope, or tactic. It's what Shakespeare is doing when he tells his loved one in Sonnet 18 that 'thy eternal beauty shall not fade'. Why? 'So long as men can breathe, or eyes can see, /So long lives this, and this gives life to thee.' (Allison 1983: 186–7). Keats plays with a similar idea in the 'Ode on a Grecian Urn'. The figures on the urn can never finish what they are doing, and the poem contains the frozenness of that moment (Allison 1983: 663–4).

In such a poem, you want the rhyme to be peaceful, clear, unthreatening, full. Even the rhyme scheme supports this notion of something being held and so preserved. If the first rhyme sound is designated A, and the next B, then we can see that Longley's stanzas rock gently between them before finishing where they began: ABABA. In the stanza above he reinforces this by rhyming on almost exactly the same word: 'turn' and 'return'. Remember what I was saying in the chapter on line about the fleeting sense we sometimes encounter, thanks to line breaks? Well here there is a similar effect through rhyme: we get the impression that the speaker of this poem would indeed like to 'turn' the boat and 'return'.

In the final stanza, rhyme is disrupted in order to demonstrate the disruption he fears will occur as a result of leaving the island: the A rhymes are far more distant. The first, 'heat', eye rhymes with 'heart', which is itself only a half rhyme for 'hurt', in that all its consonants are the same, but the vowel sound has changed. This latter rhyme is the opposite of assonance, by the way. These consonantal and assonantal rhymes are the mainstays of traditional Gaelic poetry, which we imagine might be composed on Inishmore.

So Michael Longley's use of full rhyme plays an active part in the atmosphere, mood and purpose of this poem. And so, given the departure focused on in his title, does his departure from it.

Activity 5.4   Writing

Write for 10 minutes about a journey you took in childhood. It can be something you did regularly, or only once. Concentrate on the details of the mode of transport. It may be a bicycle you owned, or your parents' first car, or the method you took to visit a relative – train, ferry, plane. Write about its appearance, its smell, the details of the route, your surroundings.

Now put rings around the keywords in the text you've produced: three or four will do. Spend 10–15 minutes on creating a Rhymewell for these, focusing on the first few 'full rhyme' ripples.

(This subsequent part can be done immediately or later, depending on how much time is available.)

Now revise the text to include as many of the rhymes as you feel fit. Try and write in lines if you haven't already done so. Don't make any special effort to put the full rhymes at the ends of lines, but don't resist if that's where they fall.

Discussion

It's difficult to fit too many full rhymes in without everything starting to chime like a children's rhyme. Of course, this is about a childhood event, so that effect is not entirely inappropriate. How bunched were your rhymes? Did you find yourself fitting in all the rhyme sounds around your keywords, or did you spread them throughout the whole text? The broader the spread, the more chance there is of happening on a rhyme-scheme like Michael Longley's – not AAA, BBB, CCC, but something more blended.

When you compose with rhyme as part of your intention from the outset, you find that you often allow the search for a rhyme to guide your composition. This can be tricky – it's generally clear when the thought in a poem has been dominated by the search for a rhyme. Of course it can also be liberating when that search throws up a word you would never have thought of otherwise. That's why the Rhymewell can be a good way of exteriorising this process and providing a broad choice.

It can be good to decide roughly on what kind of rhyme scheme you want beforehand: relying on whatever pattern starts to appear can mean struggling to insert rhyme afterwards. We'll talk more about this in the next chapter; at the moment I just want you to observe the process of working with rhyme.

As we saw in the Michael Longley poem, full rhyme is not just a decoration. It, or its absence, can contribute to the meaning of a poem. This is a subtlety not available to those who only rhyme (and only rhyme fully) because poetry 'ought' to rhyme. That's a rather useless appendage to stick on a poem, however nice it sounds. A clear meaning behind your use of full rhyme won't happen all the time, but when it does it underscores an important point: rhyme, thoughtfully deployed, is an active technique.

Slant

Slant or half rhyme appears to be a phenomenon of the last hundred years or so. In fact it is a new definition for strategies poets have always used to build up musical patterns within and across lines. In Welsh poetry, for instance, where Wilfred Owen and Dylan Thomas encountered it, it's called *proest*. It widens the focus from full rhyme to consider the range of assonantal or consonantal shapes our ear can recognise as more or less distant relations of the original rhyme sound.

In so doing it broadens the range of English, allowing it to equal the rhyming resources of Italian or Russian by drawing on its native reserves of alliteration and vowel-patterning. It also reinforces the element of discovery which is an integral part of rhyme: the surprise of a good slant rhyme will invigorate the listener's ear just as much as a too easily anticipated full rhyme wearies it.

Activity 5.5   Reading

Read 'Quoof' by Paul Muldoon (1983: 17). How many of these are full rhymes?

Quoof
How often have I carried our family word
for the hot water bottle
to a strange bed,
as my father would juggle a red-hot half-brick
in an old sock
to his childhood settle.
I have taken it into so many lovely heads
or laid it between us like a sword.

An hotel room in New York City
with a girl who spoke hardly any English,
my hand on her breast
like the smouldering one-off spoor of the yeti
or some other shy beast
that has yet to enter the language.

Discussion

This is a famous poem in which Paul Muldoon serves up another of his deft variations on the sonnet (we'll talk about the sonnet as a form in the next chapter – for now you only need to notice that there are 14 lines divided 8:6, a standard division for this form). The play of images is nicely ranged between the vivid, the unexpected and the shocking, and so are the rhymes.

There are two full rhymes here, both in the first eight lines: 'bed' and 'heads', though the latter allows itself an extra 's', and 'word' and 'sword', though the vowel sound is slightly different. Notice how putting the latter two at the beginning and end of that unit helps to hold it together.

'Bottle' and 'settle' and 'brick' and 'sock' are consonant rhymes – the vowel sounds change, but the strength of the end sounds comes through clearly. So the first four rhymes are in roughly familiar territory, just as the sense is focused on the family, its language of the hearth.

But in the six-line unit we see what happens when you fish in the further-out ripples of the Rhymewell. 'City' and 'yeti' only involve a slight vowel shift, but what a surprising rhyme. It announces the increasing distance of the speaker from his origins. 'Breast' and 'beast' is (you'll recognise this by now) another eye rhyme. The most unusual rhyme, however, is the one Muldoon chooses to finish the poem with: 'English' and 'language'.

At one level this is a deeply satisfying rhyme: 'English' is after all the 'language' which has given its speakers so much poetry. But then we remember this is an Irish poet, from a culture which had its own language suppressed in favour of English. We note that the girl, whose breast is the focus of that bizarre imagistic leap whereby hot water bottle and yeti footprint confront each other, 'spoke hardly any English'. And we realise the eroticised absurdity of teaching a non-English speaker a purely private word. Of course by this point, 'quoof' no longer feels quite so strange to us, and so we realise that this is one way of describing the 'shy beast' we have just encountered in the act of '[entering] the language'.

The complexity of what is happening in this short poem is matched by the way the rhymes approach and recede from a 'standard' notion of full rhyme. Yet again, the sound of the poem reinforces its sense; the poem attempts the greatest possible harmony between form and content.

Activity 5.6   Writing

Since this exercise is related to the one you did in Activity 5.4, let's stick with the idea of travel. Write for 15 minutes about a journey that parallels the childhood one. This time, set it in adulthood, and write about a journey either frequently undertaken, or taken once that struck you forcibly. If you like you can try and find one that parallels the childhood journey in feel – perhaps it's even the same journey, but undertaken recently.

Again, select the three or four keywords, and, when you do your Rhymewells this time, look for those more distant, more surprising rhymes.

Again, rewrite the piece, setting it in lines and attempting to incorporate as many of the more slant rhyme words as you feel will enhance the sense. Think about how you distribute them, both in the line and throughout the poem.

Discussion

Did you generate a lot of terms in each case, or did one search dominate? Was there a temptation to embellish the piece to include the more interesting rhymes, or were there rhymes you liked but just couldn't fit in?

Remember you don't need a lot of rhymes to bind a poem together – Muldoon uses just seven, each repeated once. So whether you're using full rhyme or not, you don't need to lather it on. Having said that, look at how many times within his lines you find words with '-y' or '-ly' endings: 'family', lovely', 'hardly', 'shy' – and these sounds go through the whole poem supporting it structurally.

Look at the two pieces you've written in these exercises. Do you feel that either one of them should be in full rhyme or slant rhyme? Do you feel they ought to rhyme at all? Perhaps a gentler, assonantal pattern would have suited better, or a robust, alliterative shape? At the end of this chapter look over all the pieces you've been working on, and start making notes about what sorts of sounds you'd like them to make.

Slant rhyme is to full rhyme what jazz chords are to standard guitar chords: it provides a richer texture if not the full resolution of a perfect rhyme. For this reason, it is a method of rhyming favoured by those drawn to subtlety and nuance.

Another strength slant rhyme provides is within the poem. Whether you rhyme overtly or not, these kinds of rhymes can recur, quietly, within the lines. They reinforce the framework of the poem.

Comic

When a poetic device signals its presence too strongly the effect is often comic. This is as true of rhyme as it is of far-fetched imagery or over-emphasised rhythm. Dwelling insistently on a single rhyme sound, or producing full polysyllabic rhymes, are devices a listener finds funny almost before a reader is aware of them. The impression that poetry always ought to be serious, or focused on 'important' feelings, means that some writers try to avoid such effects entirely (though over-seriousness too can bring on the giggles).

This is to overlook one of the great pleasures of poetry: that it entertains purely through its power to shape language. The listener is immediately aware when the rhythms and sounds of a poem are fresh and lively, and comic verse not only has as long a lineage as lyric poetry, if done well it communicates this liveliness in a highly direct manner.

Whether you think of yourself as funny or not, playing with language is in itself an invaluable learning process, and the comic rhyme is a powerful tool to that end.

Activity 5.7   Reading

Read the two poems 'The Shrimp' and 'The Axolotl' by Ogden Nash, from *Everyone but Thee and Me* (1968 [1963]: 67, 74). What impact does the rhyming have on the humour?

The Shrimp
A shrimp who sought his lady shrimp
Could catch no glimpse,
Not even a glimp.
At times, translucence
Is rather a nuisance.

The Axolotl
I've never met an axolotl,
But Harvard has one in a bottle,

Perhaps – and at the thought I shiver –
The very villain from Fall River,
Where Lizzie Borden took an axolotl
And gave her mother forty whaxolotl.

Discussion

I know, they're deeply silly, but allow them to speak to you out of those absurd depths. Nash is a master of the polysyllabic rhyme, where it is the very exactness of the match, syllable for syllable, which draws your attention to its absurdity. That act of drawing attention to itself is very characteristic of comic verse: in terms of its shape and its sound it's always pointing out that it's just a construct, and a rather throwaway one at that.

(Or is it? Look at the limerick, which these Nash poems resemble – everyone knows where the rhymes go, but try scanning one to find out where the heavy stresses are. Here's one I prepared earlier:

Said **I**sambard **King**dom Bru**nel**,
who **frequently visited Hell**,
'The **noise** and the **heat**
are **right** up my **street**,
but **what** they can't **get** is the **smell**.'

It's a highly complicated little form, and yet everyone seems to be able to make one up. Why? For the sheer delight of it, an important reason for writing often overlooked. Have a go.)

It's a particularly delightful anticipation we get on hearing the line 'Lizzie Borden took an axolotl', because we know what the next line will be, but we can't believe anyone would be so daft as to write it down. And yet that is the challenge we set ourselves every time we write. There's always a part of ourselves saying, 'This is daft,' and there's always another part of ourselves which has to find the gumption (courage is too serious a term) to write it down anyway. So, comic poetry touches on something quite close to the heart of the compositional process.

Nash is clearly a writer deeply in love with language, with its quirks of expression and expectation. That is why he's able to turn the comic rhyme on its head in 'The Shrimp' and, instead of a polysyllable, cut into a

121

word for the exact term (you've never wondered, but now you know) for the sightings hoped for by a frustrated male shrimp who 'Could catch no glimpse/not even a glimp.'

And of course he demonstrates admirably that in poetry the structural equivalent of the punch line is the polysyllabically rhyming couplet: its role summative, its position delayed to just the right moment, its rhyme only too anticipate-able, and its effect excruciatingly absurd.

Activity 5.8   Writing

Look at your previous Rhymewells. There should be at least seven of them, and possibly as many as nine. I'd like you to pick from them the most incongruous words, the ones that have least in common with each other. Take two words from each well. These will resemble each other, but don't have to rhyme fully. Try to come up with one full rhyme for each word. You now have the rhyme words of at least seven four-line stanzas.

Pick a mode of transport you've always wanted to use, be that gondola or yak express. Your task, which you should spend at least 15 minutes on, is to describe a journey by this mode of transport in a poem which deploys as many of these rhymes as possible. You may end up with seven stanzas, or you could decide to use only a couplet from each Rhymewell (which would produce a sort of a sonnet), or you may end up with something shorter still.

Discussion

As you've probably gathered, there's no particular need for this poem to make much sense. In this case as in many others, it's not the getting somewhere, it's the travelling that counts.

The need to bring in the seemingly irrelevant material generated by your rhyme words can create a bizarre narrative. That doesn't mean it'll be funny. Neither can the presence of odd rhymes alone guarantee a laugh – we can't all be cursed (blessed?) with the famously dreadful rhythmic sense of McGonagall.

Sometimes the material this exercise generates is more disturbing than comic. When you allow yourself to be almost entirely guided by rhyme it can be a little like free association: you're never sure what will come up next. That can be interesting. We don't always let ourselves open up when we're writing, and pursuit of the comic is one way around that restraint.

One issue that the attempt to produce comic verse usually throws up is the need for rhythmic control – jokes are all about timing, and a couplet won't have its maximum impact if you can't get both lines to move in a fluent pattern. In order to explore this, we need to move on to a study of what forms like the couplet are built out of: metre.

Comic verse encourages play with language, with ideas, and with your sense of the poet's role. It's a way of relaxing into that role, and it sometimes leads to more serious discoveries because we're relaxed: our sense of high purpose is off duty, and interesting material can slip under the radar. Playing with language is what all writers do when they're looking for new expressions; whether you're naturally funny or not, exploring such issues as complex rhyme, timing and the couplet can only have positive results.

References

Allison, A.W. *et al.* (eds) (1983) *The Norton Anthology of Poetry* (3rd edn). New York: Norton.

Curtis, Tony (ed.) (1996) *How Poets Work*. Bridgend: Seren.

Longley, Michael (1998) 'Leaving Inishmore', in *Selected Poems*. London: Cape.

Muldoon, Paul (1983) 'Quoof', in *Quoof*. London: Faber and Faber.

Nash, Ogden (1968 [1963]) *Everyone but Thee and Me*. London: J.M. Dent & Sons.

Part 2

Dialogue: Douglas Dunn (DD) and Bill Herbert (BH)

BH: Lots of people starting to write are very curious as to how poets actually make decisions, and rhyme is one of those areas in which the decision-making process seems especially mysterious to them. How do you go about distinguishing in your practice between a poem that you feel should rhyme and one that shouldn't rhyme?

DD: Well it's instinctive of course, but if you've read a lot of poetry, if you've been practising and are well-rehearsed in writing verse, then it becomes increasingly less instinctive the older you get. Poetry it seems to me should happen between the ears, there should be intelligence, intellect, originality of thought and so on. It should also happen behind the left nipple, heart, emotion, feeling – you expect that just as much as intelligence – and it should also happen between tongue and teeth, the poem should make a noise. So the part of poetry that I think we're talking about – rhyme and metre and so on – these are all part of what happens between tongue and teeth: the audibility of poetry.

BH: So there is a sense in which we're talking about the whole sound, the whole music of a poem and, again, when we think of writers starting off there's often a sense that rhyme is something that occurs discretely within a poem, rather than being part of that whole music. That seems to me to lead us into the idea of full rhyme, because the most common perception of full rhyme is of something which happens only at the end of a line. Could you talk a wee bit about how music permeates a poem for you?

DD: As it happens, English is not a particularly rich language when it comes to rhyme if you compare it with Russian, Slavonic languages in general, or especially Italian and to some considerable extent French. In English we tend to rhyme on monosyllables, and that does somehow emphasise the fullness of the rhyme because it's a short word, one syllable. Also you want the rhyme to be on a significant word. You can emphasise a meaning with rhyme and I enjoy using it, but not necessarily full rhyme all the time. The poem is called 'You'. It's a nasty and unforgiving and vindictive little poem:

> You won't believe it. Perhaps you're too prosaic
>   To fall for a poetic ache,
> But your smile (when you smile), your eyes, your nose
>   Are far too beautiful for prose
>
> Don't credit this, my dear, if you don't want to.
>   A poem, too, can be a pack of lies.
> But if you don't, then I'll come back and haunt you.
>   You'll find me hard to exorcise.

I think in contemporary poetry it's almost encouraged to vary the rhyme.

BH: It's almost a sense that the rhyme can be seen as something decorative, particularly full rhyme, that it's not got a fundamental role in forwarding or consolidating the meaning of the poem. I think what you're saying is very much that everything in the poem has to be activated, it has to be towards an end, and, in that sense, the decision between full rhyme and a more slant rhyme: is that something which happens still instinctively or is there a kind of a set of deliberations there?

DD: I think it is instinctive. It also gives an opportunity to a poet to encourage a more subtle music, one that is not exactly dissonant or off key – and I think the musical terms there are significant – but one that is more muffled. Just in the same way as many contemporary poets when they write metrically often tend to muffle the metronomic sounds of the lines, they do the same with rhyme. I think one of the first poets to use these slant rhymes as you're calling them, part rhymes or half rhymes . . .

BH: What would be your preferred term?

DD: Well, an incomplete rhyme . . . [Laughter]

BH: No implication of inadequacy there?

DD: No, not necessarily. One of the first poets to use this kind of rhyme was writing under extreme pressure of feeling and disgust and vulnerability and that was the First World War poet – Wilfred Owen. If I might just give you an example for his famous poem 'Strange Meeting' –

> It seemed that out of battle I escaped
> Down some profound dull tunnel, long since scooped
> Through granites which titanic wars had groined.
> Yet also there encumbered sleepers groaned
> Too fast in thought or death to be bestirred.

That's enough. 'Escaped', 'scooped'. The vowels don't coincide. 'Groined', 'groaned'. But there we have an effect on the 'gr' – and of course if you're a Scot you have a rhotic 'r': grroined, grroaned. It helps if you can pronounce the 'r'. In the past, in Tennyson say or in Browning or in Swinburne these would not have been considered rhymes, they would have been considered inept stabs at a rhyme. But with the advent of modernity, of modernism, this subtler kind of music and language became not just accepted but necessary.

125

BH: It certainly gives poets in English something of the flexibility which poets in say Russian or Italian have with such a broad selection of full rhyme. But with only the vowel changing and usually the consonant being preserved, that is still quite a technically demanding rhyme.

DD: Yes, well, quite a few contemporary poets use this Owenesque kind of rhyme, especially Seamus Heaney, and these muffled or incomplete rhymes are an essential part of Heaney's very distinctive music. That's why poets use rhyme: first of all it's mnemonic and it helps a poem be audible (and metre serves the same function), but it's also a test of the poet's skill, and it contributes towards the musicality of the poem. There all kinds of music as you know, as Philip Larkin said there's a kind that comes in through the ear like honey and there's the kind that comes in like broken glass. But perhaps that's what he's trying to suggest: a dissonance . . .

BH: So we're returning to the use of rhyme as opposed to the decorative . . .

DD: . . . a very expressive use of rhyme. You get it in such poets as Sylvia Plath and her poem 'Daddy', with this insistent rhyme throughout the poem – but used opportunistically, it's not regularised – on the sound 'oo'.

BH: How much largesse do you allow yourself in your work in terms of the range of rhyme? If we think about moving from full to Owenesque part rhyme, and onto the almost rococo rhyme that you get in people like Muldoon, do you feel that's a complete vocabulary that you use, or would you have restrictions?

DD: Well, I have some restrictions with this rococo rhyme which you mentioned, mainly because, like Paul Muldoon, I have a pretty dedicated taste in Lord Byron, and his poem 'Don Juan' is one of the great virtuoso examples of tremendously adroit rhyming: double syllable rhymes and triple syllable rhymes which you get for tremendous comic effect. One of my favourites is that he rhymes 'Don Alfonso' with 'does go on so'. These rhymes are hilarious and contribute enormously to the persona . . .

BH: I wanted to come on to comic rhyme, because I think that there's an interesting area in Scottish poetry in particular with this use of double and triple rhyme which we get in the Burns stanza, and of course you've written in the Burns stanza, and in other forms which use this. But I notice in your work that there is also a comedy of tone in which rhyme plays almost no part, and I'm just wondering how you feel about the use of this heavy percussive comic effect, the almost slapstick use of rhyme in Scots. Is that something you would say has a more minor role in your work or is it something that has a very particular space?

DD: A relatively minor role in my work, I think. Traditional Scots poetry especially in the Scots language is very much in your face, it's very forthright and very direct – I tend not to be that kind of person, I'm a little bit more withdrawn. Though I admire and love Burns and Ferguson and especially the earlier poets such as Dunbar and Henryson and so on. 'Extra Helpings' is a poem about school dinners. Not a very poetic subject you may feel but in the primary school I went to lunch – or dinner – was always or usually very fine. The poem is rhythmically conceived as being close to nursery rhymes:

> In our primary school
> Set lunch was the rule
> Though in Scotland we call that meal 'dinner'.
> We tucked in like starvelings,
> Inchinnan's wee darlings,
> And it didn't make thin children thinner.
>
> But what I liked best
> Was disliked by the rest,
> Rice pudding with raisins and bloated sultanas,
> Stewed fruit and dumplings
> In big extra helpings
> And hooray for first post-War bananas
> *It was very good scoff*
> *So I polished it off*
> > *A very dab hand with a spoon,*
> > *a spoon,*
> > *A very dab hand with my spoon.*

BH: Do you think that the British audience in general is a little more reluctant to take the kind of heavy slapstick that, as you described it, the Scots use of rhyme can induce?

DD: I don't know. The poet Thomas Hood – he was part Scots – was a tremendously inventive comic rhymer. And the English Edward Lear, Lord Byron – he was part Scots too.

BH: I suppose my question is do they get pushed to one corner of the canon? Is the kind of romantic lyric position still seen as occupying the central place in poetry, and does this comic rhyme have a role? Is it seen as a lesser form of poetry?

DD: Well, I think light verse in the twentieth century has been, not ridiculed, but given a certain place which I think is a great pity because many of the outstanding twentieth century poets in English had a very marked sense of humour and that's true of some contemporary poets too. I think of Carol Ann Duffy who has some poems which really make you laugh out loud; Liz Lochhead, another poet whose more cabaret performance shows tremendous technique and skill but also a very marked sense of humour; Edwin Morgan has a very marked sense of humour it seems to me. There's lots of humour in twentieth-century writing but I think by and large light verse has had a bad press.

BH: One of the great dangers that I think someone who's beginning to write poetry experiences when they try and handle rhyme is that they get led by the rhyme, that it takes them to more predictable ideas or expressions. Now of course that's the flip side of a very good coin: Yeats's famous remark that his poems came from looking for the next rhyme is about how rhyme actually makes you think differently. Do you have any tips or insights into that journey that every writer has to take from being led by the rhyme to being led in a positive sense to a new place?

DD: When a writer is beginning and they're thinking of rhyme and metricality, they can allow these techniques to lead them away from their own voice. Getting yourself into a position to identify your own voice, your physical voice, and being happy with it, is one of the things you have to do simultaneously with this acquisition of fluency and metrical writing and developing a resourcefulness in finding rhymes. You have to do these things at the same time, not separate from each otherwise you're writing for the page, or you're encouraging a false voice in yourself rather than the one that you've got by simple inheritance and environment.

BH: That leads us on to the interrelation of the rhyme and the form. It's very difficult to write a rhyming poetry that has got no understanding of metre or rhythm but a lot of people attempt this . . .

DD: . . . that's what's called doggerel. [Laughter] Rat rhyme, crambo clink. When a rhyme is delivered at the end of a falsely measured line, a metre – metre just means measure. The trick is to find your own voice. I have a terrible granny's expression, you know, 'finding your own voice', but if you think of it literally, there's no other way to put it. Rhyme can be a very friendly crutch because, if nothing else, at least you know the noise you have to make at the end of either the next line or the one after, depending on your rhyme scheme or perhaps you're writing in a stanza. I encourage students to begin their practice of rhyme by writing in very simple stanzas: quatrains, even in ballad forms.

BH: How do you go about working in more complex stanzas – I don't mean set, inherited stanzas, I mean devised stanzas. Is it a process of improvisation, or do you have set goals that you're exploring? For instance, when Grey was writing his odes there was a very definite structure that he was obviously exploring to see what kind of things he could get out of it. What's your practice?

DD: When it comes to these stanzas which you invent it's very hit or miss, it's very much a question of discovering the stanza in the process of writing. Of discovering a rhyme scheme and then perhaps the desire to regularise it – perhaps the desire not to, but to be more opportunistic. There are so many different kinds of stanza that, after practice, you can find your form quite quickly. I find that anyway. Early on it's a little bit more laborious and the temptation I think is to opt for inherited stanzas. There really aren't very many of them though, and some of them are fiendishly difficult. I don't know if you've ever tried writing in Spenserian stanzas? Good grief! [Laughter] They're enough to turn you blue.

BH: Isn't there a useful tip for the beginner here, because it's one of those funny commonplaces that you find people are constantly trying to teach students to write, say, sestinas – where you've got the fullest rhyme of all, the simple repetition of the word – when it's a very difficult form and they're at a stage in their writing abilities when they're not really going to be up to it. Would you steer them away from this?

DD: I would, absolutely. These are things that you can start trying out once you've had a bit of practice in simpler forms. I had a student last year who in the very first week said, 'Could you teach me how to write a pantoum?' I've never written a pantoum in all my born puff . . . [Laughter] I have no intention of writing a pantoum. I think this business with poetic form can be taken too far, can lead the poet away from his or her voice and away from what they really want to do in poetry. They can become sidetracked, distracted by what they feel is the necessity to learn these things. I think it's best to begin by learning blank verse, unrhymed iambic pentameter – the form of the verse of Shakespeare's plays, and of course it's got a longer history than that. It's one of the most serviceable and versatile forms and it's really quite easy to acquire. Then the poet should try writing rhyming couplets. Then simple quatrains rhyming ABAB, and then they should begin to experiment with different lengths of lines: iambic tetrameter, four beats in the line as opposed to five. How a poet rhymes will depend rather on how he or she speaks; on accent, intonation. For example, as Tony Harrison points out in one of his poems, 'matter' for Wordsworth was a full rhyme with water: 'waater'. So in this poem of mine, 'Loch Music', which in a sense is an elegy for my father, there are rhymes which I can get away with a Scots accent but which probably wouldn't be appropriate for an English speaker:

> I listen as recorded Bach
> Restates the rhythms of a loch.
> Through blends of dust and dragonflies
> A music settles on my eyes
> Until I hear the living moors,
> Sunk stones and shadowed conifers,
> And what I hear is what I see,
> A summer night's divinity.
> And I am not administered
> Tonight, but feel my life transferred
> Beyond the realm of where I am
> Into a personal extreme,
> As on my wrist, my eager pulse
> Counts out the blood of someone else.
> Mist-moving trees proclaim a sense
> Of sight without intelligence;
> The intellects of water teach
> A truth that's physical and rich.
> I nourish nothing with the stars,
> With minerals, as I disperse
> A scattering of quavered wash
> As light against the wind as ash.

It's quite difficult to write rhyming iambic tetrameter couplets, but very engaging and pleasurable once you get going. And one of the things that metre and rhyme are there for is to give the poet pleasure while he or she is working on a poem the subject of which may be anything but pleasurable.

BH: The rhetorical satisfaction of getting sound and sense in one place, is what rhyme, and I suppose couplet rhyme above all, does: it can induce a sense of the completeness of thought. So, to refer back to that moment when you make the transition from blank verse into rhyming verse, there's something that you're trying to teach them at that point as a writer . . .

DD: You're trying to teach them control of the substance of their art, which is language, simple as that. And then you can go on to try to impart finer degrees of control, more intricate control. At the same time you never want a student to lose touch, not just with his or her physical voice, but with their imaginations, the power to invent, so, as in any kind of art, an awful lot of things are going on at the same time. I think that one of the things that a beautiful artistry in a poem does to a reader is entertain. I think readers do enjoy little tricksy bits or unexpected rhymes – oh my, I didn't know that rhyme before – although it's going to be a very rare poet who finds a rhyme that hasn't been used already. Michael Longley has a poem in which he talks towards the end of being the last poet in Europe to find a rhyme. [Laughter] That has my full sympathy I can assure you. I warm to that.

BH: So if you were to think about the role of rhyme in the broader context of bringing a writer into the first flowering, the first range of their ability, is it possible to overestimate it, should it actually be downplayed? Is it a minor part of the talents which they must acquire, or do you feel that it's central?

DD: I think it's a very important part, very important indeed. If you went to the conservatory to continue studies and play the piano, I don't think anyone is going to encourage you to stop practising your scales. You have skills to learn, and these are necessary for that moment when you really do have something terribly important for you to say. At which point you've got an armoury, you've got the skills to do it, and that's very important. There's no point in relying on some sort of God-given free verse. [Laughter] I don't think God does give free verse. I don't think God likes free verse.

References

Dunn, Douglas (2003) 'You', in *New Selected Poems: 1964–2000*. London: Faber and Faber, p. 332.

Dunn, Douglas (2003) 'Extra Helpings', in *New Selected Poems: 1964–2000*. London: Faber and Faber, p. 274.

Dunn, Douglas (2003) 'Loch Music', in *New Selected Poems: 1964–2000*. London: Faber and Faber, p.108.

Owen, Wilfred, 'Strange Meeting', in *The Norton Anthology of Poetry*, 3rd edn. New York and London: W.W. Norton, 1983, p. 1035.

6

Form

By form I mean the related areas of metre and stanza. Together these constitute one of the most imposing aspects of poetry. Many people are suspicious of the assumed rigidity of a metric pattern, or the confines of often elderly stanza shapes. There is a natural tendency in the beginner to stick with free verse, and even to associate it with modernity, a relaxation of complicated rules supposed to be no longer necessary.

This is a valid position, if based on experience. We occupy a pluralistic era in which many types of poetry are possible. But if we are to be honest, then our decisions as to what forms we employ must result from open-minded examination of all the possibilities.

You may be nervous about form, but poetry is a matter of practice before theory. By attempting it, you can only strengthen your voice; by avoiding it, you only protect your writing from an unknown quantity. The unknown always tends to be more alarming than the familiar.

Certain rhythmic patterns are built into our literary heritage, but the reason to examine them is not that they are traditional, but because they enable us to do something with language that can only be approximated by other means. This is the same argument I've been advancing in relation to earlier chapters: formal issues are not dead weight, but living strategies for writing well. Feel free to disagree – cogently, giving reasons, in your journal – after all, there are no absolute rules in poetry.

But there are some very strong patterns. We ignore them at our peril, or rather at our art's peril.

These rhythmic patterns we group under the general heading of 'metre'. Metre isn't a metronomic structure we must adhere to, but something that grounds the rhythmic fluidity of the voice, something voice reacts against as well as with, something that enables sonority and stress to become measurable and memorable. We all have heartbeats, but all our hearts beat in different ways at different times. Nonetheless all these heartbeats correspond to a single governing principle: da **dum** da **dum** da **dum**.

Iambic pentameter

So, what exactly is an iambic pentameter? An old student friend, who, as he was studying law, had little interest in poetic debate, would always cite the following: 'I think I'd rather like a cup of tea.' To put the stresses in:

I **think** / I'd **rath** / er **like** /a **cup** / of **tea**

Ten syllables and five little stress patterns, or feet, each going da **dum**. (The da **dum** is the iamb, and 'penta' is from the Greek for 'five'.) Try saying it any other way, or rather, try inverting the position of the stresses: '**I** think **I'd** rath**er** like **a** cup **of** tea.' You can get away with the first two, but the rest sound decidedly odd. So iambic pentameter follows the stresses that English naturally makes.

All those stressed sounds aren't equally weighted. Said with no particular emphasis, there is nonetheless a tendency to stress some words more than others – personally I'd stress '**rath**er' a little more than '**like**', and '**cup**' and '**tea**' more than '**think**'. But for the purposes of measuring the line we only need to find two categories: stressed and unstressed. In fact, that tends not to be the difficult bit: it's not hard to tell that both 'i**am**bic' and 'pen**ta**meter' are stressed on the second syllable. The problematic part in writing pentameter is what we do with all the unstressed syllables in between.

Consider rephrasing the sentence 'English poetry is full of iambic pentameters' as an iambic pentameter. With its stresses in, it's:

English / **po**etry / is **full** / of **iamb** / ic pen**ta**meters

That's got five beats, but it's not iambic. And it's 15 syllables long, not 10. And the first stress goes **dum** da, the second goes **dum** da da. Then there's an iamb, da **dum**; and the next one goes da da **dum**. I don't even want to think what the last one is doing. (An important point to be made here is that if you can hear those beats and count those stresses, well done. As I've said before, this is called accentual verse, and these skills will take you a long way towards writing it.)

Another point to be made is that those first four patterns are perfectly respectable feet and much poetry has been written in each of them: **dum** da is called a trochee, **dum** da da is a dactyl; da **dum** you've already been introduced to, and da da **dum** is an anapaest. There are others, but recasting the phrase so that it forms an iambic pattern is the challenge here.

A useful tip is that it isn't unusual for the first foot to be 'reversed', i.e. a trochee, so in our example 'English' could stay. A less useful tip is: never reverse the second foot, it gives too strong an impression the whole line will be trochaic, so 'poetry' would have to go – except that's a far more important word here. Of course if 'English' went, the line could begin '**Po**et / ry'. The next sound would have to be stressed, though, to re-establish the da **dum** shape. What if 'is full' is contracted to '**Po**et / ry's **full**'? That's two feet out of five, but then of course you still have 'of iambic' to follow.

Perhaps you need to know another tip: elision. When you have two vowel sounds as close to each other as 'i' and 'a', you can run one into the other, creating a diphthong, or two syllables which are pronounced as though they are one. That would give us '**Po**et / ry's **full** / of **iamb** / ic . . .' – there's no way 'pentameter' is going to fit on the end of that, so there's a temptation to slap 'feet' on the end and be done. Except that's only four beats (or tetrameter). Of course you started out with 15, so perhaps you could allow yourself to fit it into two lines?

Activity 6.1   Writing

Turn the sentence 'English poetry is full of iambic pentameters' into iambic pentameter – give yourself 10 minutes. Feel free to rephrase it while preserving the essential message of the original phrase.

Once you've done that, spend another 10 minutes coming up with iambic pentameters to describe your daily habits, along the line of my pal

James's 'cup of tea' line. These don't have to connect with each other: you're simply trying the shape on for size.

Discussion

I've spent a long time looking at iambic pentameter, not just because it's the basis of a great deal of great poetry in English but because, frankly, it's difficult. Complicated from the outside, and no less complicated from the inside, but actually rather hands-on stuff. You just have to get down to it and cast and recast your lines till they sound like you.

Don't be tempted into distorting the way you would normally order a sentence. Don't worry if you have an extra unstressed syllable at the end. This, which is rather outrageously known as a feminine ending, is permissible. Just keep playing with the phrasing until you get something that will sit. Each pentameter is unique, individual, and will reflect your taste and personality if you infuse it with enough of yourself.

Here's what I ended up with:

> **I**amb**i**c **ceil**idhs **fill** our **Eng**lish **hall**
> till **these** five-**foot**ed **dan**cers **climb** its **wall**.

The iambic pentameter is something you can spend the rest of your life mastering. It is much more flexible than its detractors give it credit for – usually because they haven't spent long enough trying to write it to qualify them to judge. And if you can get the hang of it, then writing in any other metre becomes far less difficult. One reason for acquiring competence is that you can then tackle a wide variety of stanza structures and poetic forms – the sonnet, the sestina, the villanelle – which are usually written in iambics.

The various tips I mentioned above contribute to that flexibility, so I'll recap them here:

- You can reverse the first foot – and the third or the fourth (though probably not all in the same line) – without disturbing the iambic beat too much.
- Reversing the second and the fifth make it harder for the reader to hear what's happening. So don't.
- You can elide vowels if they run together and are unstressed (in fact

you can slip the occasional extra unstressed syllable in if you think you can get away with it – many do).

- And you can have an eleventh syllable at the end of the line if it's unstressed.

Of course you can decide to write in the more loosely stress-based line of accentual verse, and still work in complex forms; you can choose to write in free verse and work in them. But if you've got a notion of metre, you have a method of gauging what works or doesn't work at the rhythmic level. Look at the rhythmic pattern of the poems I've included in earlier chapters as examples. Look at the work you've produced so far.

Free

Many beginners' adoption of free verse is based on the misconception that it is not itself a form. In fact, each piece of free verse constitutes a unique form. Its rhythms, its line lengths, its shape, all demonstrate the rules of this particular form. One consequence of this is that the reader has to learn how each piece of free verse works through the act of reading. So good free verse is always simultaneously revealing its content and teaching us about its form.

This is an important skill for any writer to master. To consider the reader's reactions to this line-ending, or that indentation or spacing, to try to anticipate their thought processes, objectifies your methods and can help the process of communication.

Some free verse does not operate on these terms. Its intention is more to capture the movement of the poet's mind, in the belief that this is a more organic shape than established forms. As such, it is less concerned with its reader, and can be linked to a preference for the first draft, and a belief in inspiration. There are times when the results prove this to be an entirely valid approach, but it should not become the only model you employ. The apparently organic shape, when analysed, sometimes contains all the elements of formal verse, but in an unconsidered and even poorly constructed state.

Activity 6.2   Reading

Read 'Mr and Mrs Scotland are Dead' by Kathleen Jamie, from *The Queen of Sheba* (1994: 37). See if you can find a rhythmic pattern (note, if it exists, it might not be especially regular).

Mr and Mrs Scotland are Dead
On the civic amenity landfill site,
the coup, the dump beyond the cemetery
and the 30-mile-an-hour sign, her stiff
old ladies' bags, open mouthed, spew
postcards sent from small Scots towns
in 1960: Peebles, Largs, the rock-gardens
of Carnoustie, tinted in the dirt.

Mr and Mrs Scotland, here is the hand you were dealt:
fair but cool, showery but nevertheless,
Jean asks kindly; the lovely scenery;
in careful school-room script –
The Beltane Queen was crowned today.
But Mr and Mrs Scotland are dead.

Couldn't he have burned them? Released
in a grey curl of smoke
this pattern for a cable knit? Or this:
tossed between a toppled fridge
and sweet-stinking anorak: Dictionary for Mothers
M:— Milk, the woman who worries . . .;
And here, Mr Scotland's John Bull Puncture Repair Kit;
those days when he knew intimately
the thin roads of his country, hedgerows
hanged with small black brambles' hearts;
and here, for God's sake, his last few joiners' tools,
SCOTLAND, SCOTLAND, stamped on their tired handles.

Do we take them? Before the bulldozer comes
to make more room, to shove aside
his shaving brush, her button tin.
Do we save this toolbox, these old-fashioned views

addressed, after all, to Mr and Mrs Scotland?
Should we reach and take them? And then?
Forget them, till that person enters
our silent house, begins to open
to the light our kitchen drawers,
and performs for us this perfunctory rite:
the sweeping up, the turning out.

Discussion

In an interview in *Sleeping with Monsters*, Kathleen Jamie said she wasn't particularly interested in metrics (in Somerville-Arjat and Wilson 1990: 93–4), and this is theoretically a free verse poem, ranging from very long lines ('And here, Mr Scotland's John Bull Puncture Repair Kit') to quite short ones ('in a grey curl of smoke'). There's no iambic pattern being adhered to, no rhyme scheme, but when we analyse the poem for stresses, we find that there's quite a strong recurrence of four beat lines:

On the **civic** a**men**ity **land**fill **site** . . .
hanged with **small** black **bramb**les' **hearts** . . .
and per**forms** for **us** this per**func**tory **rite** . . .

Some lines are longer, more are shorter (the three-beat line is probably the main secondary length), but the four-beat line, or tetrameter, occurs regularly enough to feel like the dominant structural element in this poem. It's argued that a lot of iambic pentameters rely on a slightly weaker fifth beat to get to their formal length, so can just as easily be analysed as more loosely patterned four-beat lines. Perhaps Jamie's poem is not that far from pentameter.

The point is that a notional rhythmic norm can be uncovered, and this norm contributes to the poem's effectiveness. When the poem stretches to a full five beats, 'and **here**, for **God**'s sake, his **last** few **join**ers' **tools** . . .', there's a sense of the exclamation defining something rhythmically as well as rhetorically. And the last line, which is in iambic tetrameter, relies on both the expectation of four beats, and the more expansive rhythm of previous lines, in order to achieve its terse, elegiac concision (there's even a hint of a half rhyme to give us the closure of the couplet):

and per**forms** for **us** this per**func**tory **rite**:
the **sweep**ing **up**, the **turn**ing **out**.

Activity 6.3   Writing

Write for 15 minutes about an ending, but not a death or the end of a love affair. Write about when you had to get rid of some object you were very fond of – a car, a typewriter, a pair of shoes. Concentrate on describing the object and what happened to it, not on your feelings. See if your emotional response can be embedded in the description, in the imagery, or in what you did immediately after disposing of the object.

Now scan what you have written, look for the heavier beats among the unstressed syllables. Is there a dominant shape, as in Jamie's poem? Could some phrases be remade to sit with this shape? Is there a range of line lengths that seem appropriate to this piece? Consider where your line endings fall: is there any principle you can establish for these?

Spend 15 minutes revising your piece in the light of this analysis.

This way of looking at what we have written allows us to analyse something we have previously been trying to do on instinct. Most writers start with instinct, and gradually approach more formal analysis – some never feel the need to get there. The question is, how much of an instinct can someone have when they haven't actually written very much poetry?

The ability to scan your work gives you an objective tool. It also helps you to revise. (Remember, you don't have to change something to make it more regular: what if you decide you want the opposite effect?) It alerts you to what is happening structurally within your verse.

Free verse isn't exactly about doing anything you like; it's about being able to tell exactly what it is a particular poem requires, and working out whether that means it should or shouldn't conform to a historical norm. If it is to depart from that norm, how are you to do this? Certainly not by failing to notice when it's actually in a quasi-regular metre.

Free verse is not an easier form than metric poetry – sometimes it's just a less considered piece of writing. But at its best it is fully conscious, able to dip in and out of tradition as it pleases, producing a unique marriage between form and content that surprises and delights the reader whether they notice its radical shape or not.

Discovered

The discovered form frequently occurs because you create a shape you like in some section of a poem, and decide you want to repeat it elsewhere, or produce a variation based on it. You can repeat a syllable pattern or roughly duplicate a line length. You can put rhymes in the same places or just divide your poem into stanzas of a similar number of lines. Whatever you do, it points to an underlying truth about metre and stanza.

We all enjoy patterns in sound, and poets actively seek them out. Poets want to make patterns, not because they don't exist elsewhere, but because the elements of pattern are already present. Metric verse and stanzaic patterns are derived forms, not imposed ones, and engagement with them is part of the same impulse that drives poets to engage with language.

Activity 6.4   Reading

Read 'The Canonization' by John Donne, from *The Complete English Poems* (1971: 47). How neatly do the sentences (and Donne's argument) fit firstly into the lines and then into the stanzas?

The Canonization
For God's sake hold your tongue, and let me love;
    Or chide my palsy, or my gout;
    My five grey hairs, or ruin'd fortune flout;
With wealth your state, your mind with arts improve;
        Take you a course, get you a place,
        Observe his Honour, or his Grace;
Or the King's real, or his stamp'd face
        Contemplate; what you will, approve,
        So you will let me love.

Alas! alas! who's injured by my love?
    What merchant's ships have my sighs drowned?
    Who says my tears have overflow'd his ground?

When did my colds a forward spring remove?
　　When did the heats which my veins fill
　　Add one more to the plaguy bill?
Soldiers find wars, and lawyers find out still
　　Litigious men, which quarrels move,
　　Though she and I do love.

Call's what you will, we are made such by love;
　　Call her one, me another fly,
　　We're tapers too, and at our own cost die,
And we in us find th' eagle and the dove.
　　The phoenix riddle hath more wit
　　By us; we two being one, are it;
So, to one neutral thing both sexes fit.
　　We die and rise the same, and prove
　　Mysterious by this love.

We can die, by it, if not live by love,
　　And if unfit for tombs or hearse
　　Our legend be, it will be fit for verse;
And if no piece of chronicle we prove,
　　We'll build in sonnets pretty rooms;
　　As well a well-wrought urn becomes
The greatest ashes, as half-acre tombs,
　　And by these hymns, all shall approve
　　Us canonized for love;

And thus invoke us; "You whom reverend love
　　Made one another's hermitage;
　　You, to whom love was peace, that now is rage;
Who did the whole world's soul contract, and drove
　　Into the glasses of your eyes;
　　So made such mirrors, and such spies,
That they did all to you epitomize—
　　Countries, town, courts beg from above
　　A pattern of your love."

Donne, John (1971) 'The Canonization' in John Donne: *The complete English poems*, A.J. Smith (ed.), Harmondsworth: Penguin, p. 47.

Discussion

This is the only non-contemporary poem I will ask you to consider, and I do so for a combination of reasons. Firstly, Donne is a great master of stanza forms, giving the impression he improvises his first stanza's shape, then effortlessly reproduces the same pattern. He has an almost unique ability to make the iambs fit his voice; his poetry is full of idiomatic energy, even if that idiom is from a different era. Secondly, when I was 16 I was taught Donne by a very good teacher: this is a poem which made a huge impact on me when I began writing. Because of that I still think of Donne as an excellent model to begin with when looking at formal verse. He thinks, brilliantly, and feels, intensely, and his form matches the movement of thought and the emotional range, precisely.

The poem opens with an outburst, which dismisses the whole of the go-getting world in a single sentence, ending with the same key word that ends the first line: 'love'. He then keeps that repetition up for four more stanzas, obliging himself to find 10 rhymes for love (in fact he finds eight, and repeats two – nobody's perfect, or rather, not every-one needs to pretend they're perfect). In the course of this he considers sexual mores, myth and contemporary thought, ending with the outrageous conceit that he and his lover are sufficiently emblematic of Love to become saints. Let's look at the stanza form in which he does it.

The first four lines consist of pentameter (lines 1, 3 and 4), and tet-rameter (line 2); they rhyme ABBA, an envelope rhyme (where the first rhyme envelops the second), which is found in the Italian sonnet. (A traditional British rhyme for this four-line unit or quatrain is ABAB, which is how Shakespeare rhymed in his sonnets. Ballads follow this pattern, but usually don't bother with the first rhyme: if we can designate a non-rhyming sound as X, then the ballad stanza rhymes XAXA.)

The next three lines are two tetrameters (lines 5 and 6), followed by another pentameter, and these rhyme CCC. This three-line unit is called a tercet. Finally we have another tetrameter (line 7) and, to finish, a three-beat or trimeter line, and these you'll recognise as a couplet: DD.

So each stanza rhymes ABBACCCDD, and the number of feet per line is 545544543. Sounds a bit bare. But this is notating the skeleton: to appreciate the shape we have to reread the poem: notice how many times Donne uses the fuller quatrain to establish the dominant idea for that stanza, then turns to a new idea or a variation in the next three lines, bringing each movement smartly to a (temporary) conclusion in his couplets.

These three units – quatrain, tercet, couplet – enable the poet to build a range of different verse shapes, each capable of containing the flow of very different thoughts and images. Varying the length of the lines allows you to be expansive or concise. These principles are as true of accentual and free verse as of metrical pieces.

Activity 6.5   Reading and writing

Don't worry, I'm not going to ask you to write a 45-line poem in a stanza of your own devising that ranges across all of contemporary experience – you can do that later. What I am going to ask is that you attempt these building blocks: I'd like you to write three separate poems: one two lines long, one three, and one four. Try to write in metre, and rhyme, but the metre can be accentual or iambic, and the rhyme can be slant or full, as you or rather as the poem sees fit. Read the following, then give yourself 15 minutes for the exercise.

The couplet's strong summative note means it frequently ends up at the ends of poems: poems composed entirely of couplets have a hard job maintaining momentum unless each couplet is a stage in a developing argument, or you don't pause the poem at every rhyme, letting the meaning flow over. The couplet by itself must be conclusive. For this reason, poets like to write epigrams in it: short witty pieces which address a single issue or sum up a single person. Here's the Roman poet Martial as translated by Brendan Kennelly (2003: 18):

> You ask me why I like the country air.
> I never meet you there.

The tercet takes things a step further, in that the first two lines can open up an argument the third can clinch: if you want to develop an image, then comment on it, you've more room. Rhyme-wise there are a few possibilities more than the single rhyme – CCC – we found in Donne: you can rhyme first and third AXA. The most famous tercet form in Western poetry, the *terza rima* of Dante's *Divine Comedy*, follows this pattern, though in Dante the middle sound is taken up in the next stanza: ABA BCB and so on. You can have a couplet followed by a third unrhymed line, AAX, or vice versa.

Probably the best illustration of the dynamics of the tercet is non-metrical, unrhymed and non-Western: the haiku. Everyone learns the haiku as a syllabic form (5–7–5), though this is an approximate translation from an ideographic writing system. What the haiku does perfectly is observe and turn: something is seen, then, with a little shift, it is reflected on. Here's Basho (1985: 75):

> Small hut in
> summer grove, untouched
> by woodpeckers.

The quatrain is one of the most common stanza forms because it's big enough to develop an idea or image, and the even number of lines allows for a sense of balance. The number of possible rhymes is sufficiently diverse to lend some variety – not just ABBA and ABAB (or XAXA), but also two couplets, AABB, and three and one rhymes, AXAA, with the option of moving the position of the unrhymed line around, or of picking it up in a subsequent stanza (AABA BBCB). Many writers almost instinctually begin with some form of four-line stanza, usually following the ballad rhyme scheme.

The four-line poem can make a very satisfying unit for a short poem: there are many examples of this, from the Rubaiyat to Rabindranath Tagore's *kabitika* to the four-line unit in traditional Chinese poetry. Here's one by the seventh-century poet Wang Wei (1973: 31):

> I sit alone in the dark bamboos
> Play my lute and sing and sing
> Deep in the woods where no one knows I am
> But the bright moon comes and shines on me there.

The discovered form, like the slant rhyme or the unexpected line break, can give a freshness and energy to a poem. You can arrive at a range of different forms by combining the couplet, tercet and quatrain, varying the length of the lines and the rhyme-schemes. You can also copy the different shapes poets have put together, including the Spenserian stanza, Burns's Standard Habbie, Byron's *ottavo rima*, Keats's ode stanza, and Arnold's Scholar Gypsy stanza (for examples see Allison *et al.*, pp.110, 511, 592, 660 and 783). The act of combining can leave you with elaborate shapes, so start simple and build gradually towards more difficult patterns.

Selected

Increased fluency with metre and stanza encourages writers to select more complex constructions. The various shapes which have emerged in British poetry over the centuries offer us a challenge which is a key part of the whole process of composition. This is the challenge of integrating content with form. Here we'll focus on one of the most durable short forms: the sonnet.

A poem is not a vessel into which we pour a previously prepared substance. On the contrary, by working within the particular restraints of a poem, we find that its laws alter our expression. An unexpected image or a surprising rhyme create new associations, and so too the demands of a stanza form reshape our thought. This is particularly true of the sonnet: we don't write to express ourselves, we write to discover what the sonnet is saying, how it expresses us.

By electing to write in an established shape, we firstly explore how that shapes us, but we also enter into a dialogue with all previous users of that form. We begin a larger dialogue than the beginner's conversation with him- or herself, or the address to a contemporary audience: we start to speak with the dead. By addressing a tradition, we place ourselves within it, and even consider how we may be read by future audiences.

The sonnet has a complicated history, which means it has come down to us in a number of forms. Two are commonly used in poetry in English: the Petrarchan (its name reflects the form's Italian origins, Petrarch being one of its first masters), and the Shakespearean (not that he was the only Elizabethan to pen a few, but history finds it easier to simplify). Each is 14 lines long, and there is a division after the eighth line which gives us two main units, the octave and the sestet. The different ways the two kinds of sonnet rhyme affect the way ideas and arguments develop.

Activity 6.6 Reading

Read these two sonnets. The first, by Edwin Morgan, is Petrarchan; the second, by Eleanor Brown, is Shakespearean. Observe the different patterns of rhyme, and consider what impact these have on each poem's argument.

Glasgow Sonnets, i

A mean wind wanders through the backcourt trash.
Hackles on puddles rise, old mattresses
puff briefly and subside. Play-fortresses
of brick and bric-a-brac spill out some ash.
Four storeys have no windows left to smash,
but in the fifth a chipped sill buttresses
mother and daughter the last mistresses
of that black block condemned to stand, not crash.

Around them the cracks deepen, the rats crawl.
The kettle whimpers on a crazy hob.
Roses of mould grow from ceiling to wall.
The man lies late since he has lost his job,
smokes on one elbow, letting his coughs fall
thinly into an air too poor to rob.

(Morgan 1990: 289)

XLIII

He is a very inoffensive man;
a man without grave faults or dreadful tastes,
who need not be embarrassing; who can
tell an amusing anecdote; who wastes
less time than most on foolish flattery,
without descending into boorishness;
can pay a compliment quite prettily,
avoiding many kinds of clumsiness;

a very inoffensive man indeed;
an interesting man, and sensitive;
the sort that would be pleased to soothe a need,
if it were anything that he could give;
and I have sat with him this whole day through,
and hated him, because he is not you.

(Brown 1996: 40)

Discussion

Morgan's sonnet, you may notice, has fewer rhymes in it than Brown's. Italian finds it far easier to rhyme than English, and this may well be one reason why the form was changed. The structure of a Petrarchan sonnet is built around repetition of two units you're familiar with: the quatrain rhyming ABBA, and the tercet rhyming CDC. The first occurs twice in the octave, the second twice in the sestet. Morgan has started his sequence of 10 sonnets with a bravura gesture: 'mattresses' 'fortresses' 'buttresses' 'mistresses' is no mean feat of rhyming from no mean city.

(Notice that to scan this as a pentameter, the last syllable 'es' is being treated as stressed. This trick, treating an unstressed or more lightly stressed syllable as stressed in order to make up the pattern, is used quite often in metrical verse: my old favourite 'lascivious' could be scanned as 'la **scivi ous**' if need be, though you can at least hear that there's slightly more stress on 'ous' than on the preceding 'i'. Back when I was naming the parts of the phrase 'English poetry is full of iambic pentameters', this was the one I held back on: the two unstressed syllables at the end of the phrase '-eters.' It's called a pyrrhic foot.)

Of course you could allow yourself the luxury of introducing new rhymes in the second quatrain, and the sestet is sometimes rhymed CDECDE, which has the same result (also CDDCDD, which doesn't, but anticipates the Shakespearean).

Eleanor Brown's sonnet breaks down into three quatrains, rhyming ABAB, then a couplet. The fact that you don't have to repeat the rhyme means that the quatrains can be more independent units, but Brown has chosen to run her first eight lines together syntactically and repeat her opening line at the opening of the sestet, demonstrating how a Petrarchan feel can be hinted at by the Shakespearean form. However, the emotive turn of the final couplet means the 8:6 division of the Italian sonnet is set against a 4:4:4:2 formation. Yes, I know I sound like a football pundit.

The effect of this shift of emphasis to the last two lines is to make the development of a Shakespearean sonnet feel more linear. The Petrarchan can abruptly shift around the end of the octave, an effect called the *volta* or leap, like the turn in a haiku. As we see the Shakespearean is at liberty to do this too – these are flexible forms which have evolved to follow patterns of thought, and indeed to guide thought into those patterns.

Activity 6.7   Writing

Donne says in 'The Canonization' 'We'll build in sonnets pretty rooms'. I'd like you to write a sonnet about a room you've stayed in. It could be your childhood bedroom; your favourite room in your current house (even the room you're sitting in now); a room you once entered as a guest, a visitor, a tourist.

Decide which sonnet form you'd like to try out, but don't trap yourself in it: remember both forms arguably consist of three quatrains up to the last two lines, when you have to decide whether to go for a couplet or complete a tercet. Try writing in pentameter, but allow yourself the luxury of lapsing into accentual verse: this isn't a penance or a workout. Don't feel you have to rhyme – the shape's the thing in the first instance. If you want to rhyme, don't worry whether you use ABBA or ABAB rhymes – plenty of poets have mixed and matched, and you're just experimenting.

My advice is to write freely for 10 minutes, generating descriptions, images and comparisons, and then do a little bit of planning. Treat the first two quatrains as introduction and development, and the sestet as reaction and conclusion. Consider including images for things in the room; comparisons of the room with other places; accounts of things that happened in the room; contrasts between how you felt once and how you feel now. Consider fitting those various ideas into the units you've already worked with: quatrain, tercet, couplet.

Give yourself 15–20 minutes to work on the sonnet (Shelley took 15 for 'Ozymandias', quick work even for him, but it goes to show it can be done). Return to it as often as is necessary, but work in short, 15-minute bursts.

Discussion

Sonnets can be hard to fill, or hard to squash everything into, or your thought can fit one as snug as a puffin in a burrow. How was yours? Some people say 'never again', others 'I'll get it right next time'. In either case it can be years before the subject comes along that best suits both you and the sonnet.

But there's a huge satisfaction when the thoughts and the rhymes and the stanzas all cohere. There's a sense of having made something new out of an old design, and this goes close to the point of being a poet at all. The word is derived from *poesis* – Greek for making. In my tradition, Scots poets have been known as 'makars' – makers – since before the sonnet entered the language. Poetry is about making something new out of words, something shaped, unique and sturdy.

The engagement with form is the point at which writing poetry begins to be a craft, rather than just a means of self-expression. Whether that engagement is with previous forms, or the search for a new form that will contain your voice, doesn't matter. The point is that something previously incoherent has gained substance.

People begin writing by hardly noticing words, just concerning themselves with what words say. Gradually, words become substantial to them as musical, rhythmic units. Similarly, patterns of words begin to be clearer, whether those of the line or of the larger units in a poem. It becomes possible that something can be built from word and line and stanza.

The word stanza comes from the Italian for 'room': *stanze* (which is why I set that subject for the sonnet). Rooms are part of a larger structure, and this notion of the poem as house, as something habitable, is probably the most important lesson form teaches us.

References

Allison, A.W. *et al.* (eds) (1983) *The Norton Anthology of Poetry* (3rd edn). New York: Norton.

Basho, Matsuo (1985) 'Haiku No. 233', in *On Love and Barley: Haiku of Basho*, Lucien Stryk (tr.). Harmondsworth: Penguin.

Brown, Eleanor (1996) *Maiden Speech*. Newcastle upon Tyne: Bloodaxe Books.

Donne, John (1971) 'The Canonization', in *John Donne: The complete English poems*, A.J. Smith (ed.). Harmondsworth: Penguin.

Jamie, Kathleen (1994) 'Mr and Mrs Scotland are Dead', in *The Queen of Sheba*. Newcastle upon Tyne: Bloodaxe Books.

Kennelly, Brendan (2003) 'The Reason', in *Martial Art*. Tarset: Bloodaxe Books.

Morgan, Edwin (1990) 'Glasgow Sonnets, i', in *Collected Poems*. Manchester: Carcanet Press.

Somerville-Arjat, Gillean and Wilson, Rebecca E. (eds) (1990) *Sleeping*

with Monsters: Conversations with Scottish and Irish women poets.
Dublin: Wolfhound.

Wang, Wei (1973) 'Bamboo Grove House', in *Wang Wei: Poems*, G.W.
Robinson (tr.). Harmondsworth: Penguin.

Part 2

Dialogue: Sean O'Brien (SO'B) and Bill Herbert (BH)

BH: I think an interesting starting point for a lot of new writers would be to talk about how you came to metre, how you began to write the metrical as opposed to the free verse line. Is it the result of an infatuation? Is it an obsession? How did the line meet you?

SO'B: I came to writing in metre gradually and, in the early stages, without much conscious analysis of it. I started probably by writing the odd ballad. Just as simple as you can get, really, and as capacious as well. And then I did a poem called 'Victorians' which seemed to need – this is in the late seventies – that seemed to need the kind of edged certainty, the carved quality of the stanza form in order to accommodate it. And I moved in and out of thinking metrically for some time, but if I look at my early work, it's really in the early eighties, when I began to work on a poem called 'Cousin Coat', that metre became a really deliberate significant feature in what I do. It's about feeling a responsibility to history; to those you have to deal with who went before, and to go on making their case. The speaker of the poem is wearing a very heavy black overcoat which has probably been lying in the Aire Canal in Leeds for the last hundred and fifty years and just been dug out. At the same time he has always been wearing it.

Cousin Coat

You are my secret coat. You're never dry.
You wear the weight and stink of black canals.
Malodorous companion, we know why
It's taken me so long to see we're pals,
To learn why my acquaintance never sniff
Or send me notes to say I stink of stiff.

But you don't talk, historical bespoke.
You must be worn, be intimate as skin,

And though I never lived what you invoke,
At birth I was already buttoned in.
Your clammy itch became my atmosphere,
An air made half of anger, half of fear.

And what you are is what I tried to shed
In libraries with Donne and Henry James.
You're here to bear a message from the dead
Whose history's dishonoured with their names.
You mean the North, the poor, and troopers sent
To shoot down those who showed their discontent.

No comfort there for comfy meliorists
Grown weepy over Jarrow photographs.
No comfort when the poor the state enlists
Parade before their fathers' cenotaphs.
No comfort when the strikers all go back
To see which twenty thousand get the sack.

Be with me when they cauterise the facts.
Be with me to the bottom of the page,
Insisting on what history exacts.
Be memory, be conscience, will and rage,
And keep me cold and honest, cousin coat,
So if I lie, I'll know you're at my throat

That poem was really written once as what we can probably call 'free verse' and then completely rewritten in stanzas, very strictly rhyming metrical stanzas, because I came to feel that there was a sort of correlation between, not so much the poem's content, but the poem's attitude to itself and the kind of deliberation of form and possibly the authority that the form might confer.

BH: I think, when people are approaching form, when they are beginning to write in it, this is one of the things that they find difficult. Perhaps they associate it with as you say a traditional and possibly reactionary way of looking at the world, and also it comes with a lot of fear. They are intimidated by it. They think of it as something difficult and alien in some cases. How do you think people get over that? How did you come to get over that, or did you not experience it?

SO'B: I may, when I was pretty young, have felt what I think is quite commonly felt: that form in some way looked anachronistic, and in some way was associated with things that I didn't want to associate with. I think people should not confuse free verse with political liberty for example as sometimes seems to happen. But in the late 1970s I was very fortunate in having several years of informal tutoring from Douglas Dunn, who put me straight about this and many other things as well. To sum up his teaching on the subject, he indicated that form is an imaginative obligation, that a poem must be able to give an account of itself. Stand up and justify why it is the way it is. All poetry is formal to a degree; the degree of deliberation and finesse is another matter. The major thing about form in the first instance is that it is a craft skill. It is something that you have to learn how to do. It is something that you have to practise and get better at. Some people are very lucky. They have a very highly developed ear for the musicality of a line very quickly and you know good luck to them. That's great. But the rest of us actually have to learn how to get ten syllables and five stresses – to use an iambic line as the example – how to get them to actually work, to be both natural and rhetorical; to be both spoken and have some kind of imaginative consequence to them. It seems to me to be the equivalent of learning to play an instrument. It's the exercises which are necessary. In order to be able to play the piano you have to practice scales. In order to play the violin you have to practise scales. It is a craft skill and I think one of the things that has really bedevilled later modernity in our period is the intellectually very empty assumption that craft is something that people used to do and what we have now are ideas which are much superior. I think form is where the poetry really is.

BH: There is a sense that people bring to it that it is a kind of decoration. That it is not for use; that it does not have a use. I suppose that is partly a fear of counting, of being obsessive. Is there a space in which you either feel that it is an obsessive pursuit in addition to being a craft or as opposed to being a craft? I mean how strict are you when you are writing formally?

SO'B: I am pretty strict and I have a reasonably good ear although I noticed, especially in writing plays, that I quite frequently write a hexameter which I don't notice until a few lines later when something sounds slightly amiss and I go back and discover that there are 12 syllables in that line and not 10. Yes, it does play to obsession, with the idea of actually doing something right. If you accept a rule then live by it. I think, in terms of verse paragraphs or entire poems, which have a kind of accumulative, unfurling rhythm within them to which every phrase and line contributes, that there is a combination of flesh and architecture and breath that goes into the making of a poem, all of which has to sit comfortably with itself. So form is not simply an empty activity. It is not a building of decorated containers or vehicles into which meaning is placed. Form is the producer of meaning, which is of course a very ambiguous remark, because the incompetent poet ends up with meanings he doesn't want because he hasn't control of the form.

BH: Can you contrast that with free verse in any way? How does one go about deciding a poem ought to be in free verse? Are there separate criteria? How do you go about writing free verse?

SO'B: I tend – insofar as I have a firm view of it – to think that the decision is made almost before consciousness; that a particular poem just takes to form of a traditionally recognised sort and another is more of an improvisation, a weighing of one phrase against another without so much regard for line length for example or necessarily for stress counting even. There is a kind of justice of the utterance to which American poets in particular have devoted a great deal of time and effort. Somebody like Robert Creeley, whose work in itself I don't find particularly interesting, I find very interesting formally because of the absolutely meticulous fastidious determination to decide where the line break is in free verse: it will have the maximum dramatising performative effect on the poem without distorting what is speakable. I think the relation between the dramatic and the speakable has quite a lot to do with free verse when it's really working. And the authority derives from an enormous repertoire of what you might call rhythmic colourings, of selecting from them momentarily. But the mid period of somebody like Louis Simpson seems to me to be very interesting, kind of apparently conversational, anecdotal free verse that is actually very carefully weighed. You don't realise how remarkably rhetorical it is until you turn away from the poem. What you have been led to believe is just somebody talking is actually somebody working on you.

This poem is called 'A Provincial Station' and it takes place somewhere in Central Europe in perhaps the early years of the twentieth century. It is supposed to be like a little cross-section through a novel; the sort of thing that Louis Simpson wrote so brilliantly during the seventies and – I think – it's in free verse:

> The brutalised youth has returned
> With the compasses, sketch book, unhealthy ideas,
> From his motherless home or the military school,
> To stand on the clinker beside the low shed
> At one end or the other of summer.
> Grey, thundery weather, the sighing of reeds.
>
> Three days ago he left
> This very place, it seems –
> Birchwood, marshes, village out of sight.
> The train's lugubrious siren pulls away.
> Here's Kostya!
> Or whatever the hell he's called,
> In his all-weather coat made of sacking,
> Sitting in a coma in the trap,
> With the old horse, Misha,
> Dead for years, tormented by mosquitoes.

BH: If one of the main structural supports in free verse is actually rhetoric, then that's a dependency because in a formal poem you have rhetoric as well. So it is putting a lot of weight on one part of the equation. Do you think that there are other forms apart from rhetoric that free verse uses in this way? Other forms of speech rather than metric forms? What are the dangers of free verse?

SO'B: I think the danger of free verse, and it's a danger suffered by other kinds of verse as well but perhaps it is particularly exposed in free verse, is of the religiosity of the self. That the most banal apprehension is treated as if it were the annunciation of the birth of the new Christ. There is the terrible hush that surrounds the words on the page, and again I would have to say that American poets tend to be terribly guilty of this. They go in awe of their own utterances rather too readily and it's a sort of emperor's new clothes job where there isn't actually anything there really being uttered. The epiphany is really a measure of the desire to be getting on with another poem. So I think free verse is to be practised with caution, because it becomes readily very habitual. And it invites a disregard really for line and line-break even though it emphasises these things.

BH: The idea of the poet building something, constructing something points us towards the route of stanza, as in *stanze*, the room. How do you go about building these rooms within poems? Are you a stanzaic writer and do you use established ones (you talked about the ballad) or do you invent new ones? If so, how do you do that?

SO'B: I'm a stanzaic writer but I am also an improviser in that quite frequently I am looking for the kind of stanzaic justice that can be promulgated in a particular poem. Sometimes I think, yes, I see this as a poem of iambic pentameters and it will be in rhyming sestets rhyming *ABABCCC*: sometimes that is immediately apparent – something in the tone as much as anything else indicates that is how it is going to be. Sometimes, however, I am writing something which isn't rhymed and which isn't so rigorously metrical but nonetheless is very rhythmically driven. (If there is one thing that tends to characterise my work it's the rhythmically driven, even when it's not operating particularly conventionally.) So I am looking for a way of making a stanza within a long verse paragraph.

BH: Can you talk a little bit about the difference between a stanza and a verse paragraph because I think that's the sort of thing people might just think were equal.

SO'B: Let's suppose for a moment that a stanza is a self-contained item within a poem; that is grammatically closed; that it has terminal punctuation – sounds like a disease. Then I take it that in some way an argument or a pseudo-argument is being advanced from one stanza to the next: on the one hand, on the other hand, the outcome; thesis, antithesis, perhaps. In a verse paragraph it seems to me that there is likely to be more sense of turmoil, perhaps, of something being weighed and argued over as the poem goes. An attempt to bring to light something which the stanzaic poem may be finessing. But I am not trying to sell the stanza short when I say that. It's just that the angle of illumination may be different, if I can put it that way. In the stanzaic poem things tend to be offered as it were to the sun. In the verse paragraph things are in the process of emerging.

BH: The reason I was thinking about that distinction was because, when you get to a larger unit like the sonnet or a large stanza unit, then it does feel a bit like you have acquired the status of a paragraph or something like that; a larger, complete sub-section or a larger complete unit in itself. Are you someone who is drawn to the sonnet, and is that a shape that encapsulates some of these ideas for you, or is it a very different thing?

SO'B: I am interested in sonnets. I have never written one that I have found satisfactory but I have published one or two. This poem is called 'At the Wellgate' and it's a sonnet with one rhyme missing and it is set in Dundee in the depths of winter:

> Their speechless cries left hanging in the cold
> As human fog, as auditory stench,
> The boreal flâneurs donate their stains
> And thick cirrhotic sherries to the bench
> Outside the precinct where they are not allowed,
> And finding they've no stories [left] to tell
> And thus no purchase on the Christmas crowd,
> Descend by means of manholes into Hell.
>
> Which in their case is arctic and unmapped,
> Its every inch the coiling thick of it,
> As if the Piranesi of the tubes
> Had framed a labyrinth of frozen shit,
> In which they wander howling and rehearse
> The notion that elsewhere could still be worse.

I think it's a form – if I could put it this way – that I have never been able to satisfy. I either feel that I have got not enough or too much. The limits of your thinking are exposed by this in some way; that if you look at great sonnets in the tradition of which there are an awful lot, there is never any sense of something being deflated or inflated. There is a sort of natural congruence between form and utterance. And I just think that is extremely difficult to accomplish. But I am interested in the sonnet. People tend to take it as the measure of English poetry as much as they take the blank verse line, the Shakespearean or Wordsworthian line, the sonnet seems to be where – if the public has a view of these things – it is where the public thinks it's at.

BH: This makes again a point of intimidation for the new writer. There is that sense that you are up against everything before, which must make it very difficult for someone to actually embark on these. I often wonder whether the new writer should be attempting these things at all. There is a tendency to teach people things like villanelles, sestinas and sonnets, and I wonder if it does more harm than good?

SO'B: Without being a bigot about it, I quite often come across students who have been somewhere else and they have written sestinas and villanelles, and it is as if they have been subjected to a cruel and unusual punishment, and what they have produced is something which is genuinely empty. It's all container. It's all happen and no cattle. They have done it but in fact it has done them. The poem has escaped alive into the ether again. It's very difficult to write a villanelle. William Empson's variations on the villanelle, along with one or two bits of Auden, are the most interesting examples of it because Empson is having to remake this damned thing for himself. There is a tremendous sense of strain attached to it, which is more interesting than that rather empty self-satisfied mellifluousness which sometimes comes with a villanelle.

BH: Which comes back to the point I think you started with, with the metric line: that these are things which must be discovered and made afresh by the writer in the act of writing rather than going to with their cap in their hand.

SO'B: Yes. You have to just sit there for as long as it takes and you will know when you have managed to do it right, when you have managed to produce a handful of lines that actually metrically work and are natural but also do their rhetorical job. But the iambic line is fantastically diverse. It's not one thing. It's a bit like saying football is one thing. Well, yes, but there is a difference between Hartlepool United and Real Madrid, and I think you have to come in at the Hartlepool United end and work upwards to get into Europe. But also there is just the difference in sound between somebody like Dryden writing an iambic line, and somebody like Wordsworth and somebody like Keats, and then modern poets writing the iambic line. They all have their own inflexion, and it is tonal as much as anything, in the same way as great sax players' tones can be heard at a distance and you know who it is you are listening to without having to be told. There is a certain character; a certain briskness or weightiness or a lightness of touch or a sense – in Dryden's case, say – of an enormous competence, not even all being directed at this task presently.

BH: Well, that is a very interesting point because I think that you are almost saying that form is a way of searching for voice: that you move from the Scylla and Charybdis of empty rhetoric in free verse, and vacuous content in extreme closed form, towards a sense of discovering your own voice. Does that seem right?

SO'B: Yes. Or of staging your own voice if I might put it that way. I think that dramatisation has a lot to do with it. I don't mean self-dramatising hysteria. I just mean being able to enhance those aspects of your imagination as it speaks itself which are pertinent; to have a range of tones at your disposal, which will be assisted by attention to line breaks and so on. So, yes, we all know – I mean anybody who has stuck at this business long enough, has the odd occasion where you think, 'Yes I recognise that. That's me.' It doesn't happen very often but occasionally you think, 'Yes.' And often it's a surprising recognition; that you didn't quite recognise this figure who is shambling out of the tunnel with an arrow through his hat. But it is. Somehow by luck and judgement. You have just got that arrangement of syllables and noises that actually have some authority and I think authority is what I am really after.

References

O'Brien, Sean (2002) 'Cousin Coat', in *Cousin Coat: Selected Poems 1976–2001*. London: Picador, p. 44.

O'Brien, Sean (2002) 'A Provincial Station', in *Cousin Coat: Selected Poems 1976–2001*. London: Picador, p.127.

O'Brien, Sean (2002) 'At the Wellgate', in *Cousin Coat: Selected Poems 1976–2001*. London: Picador, p. 83.

7

Theme

Part 1

Theme in poetry arises from the sense that there is an area of concern to which the writer keeps returning. There may be a set of subjects we write about which, on examination, share an underlying theme. Like voice, this is better discovered than imposed, but this does not preclude the search. The attempt to address large issues or grand abstractions often occurs when a writer has little idea what they write well about. At such points they imitate the journalist searching for current or 'important' issues, rather than expressing what comes naturally to them – except that a journalist has a specific editor and audience to satisfy.

Often the subjects which engage us seem unlikely or slight, and we have to trust that inner compulsion which will eventually reveal the theme. Sometimes that theme may pass unnoticed until a reader or a fellow poet points it out. By engaging with such themes, the writer begins to move beyond the compass of a single poem, and starts to compose and revise in terms of the sequence or even the collection.

Activity 7.1   Reading

Read the extract from 'Proceedings in Palmersville' by Sean O'Brien. What is O'Brien's attitude towards his themes: precise, imprecise; matter-of-fact, respectful?

I want to write poems which are places, in which paraphraseable meaning has been drawn back into the place itself, so that the reading of the poem resembles inhabiting or at any rate contemplating the place. The original landscapes of my life – Anlaby Road, Hull, in the mid 50s; the flat behind the butcher's shop, with its garden of lilacs; Salisbury Street, with its vast, lost orchard; the tenfoots between the avenues; the riverwide greenmantled drains before they were filled in the 60s; the goods line at the back of the houses; the bodily stink of purple furnace ash and free milk in the vast yards of St Winifred's RC Infants: these are not something to use but to enter, though I don't know why. They are sufficient.

Politics is also inscribed in this material whenever I examine it, although I'm sometimes told I'm wrong by the pure in heart. This should ideally have been the sole item in this document. It would also contain railway arches, viaducts, junctions, cuttings, dead stations, torn-up lines, dockside buffers, lock-gates, estuaries, the Ouseburn, statues of De La Pole and Collingwood, lighthouses, sea-lanes, ice-bergs, places which only exist as numbers on an Admiralty chart.

(O'Brien 2000: 239–40)

Discussion

Notice how O'Brien's impulse to compose is concerned with physical objects in a definite landscape – there is a strong sense of political engagement, and an effort to recover the past, and these two elements are linked. His work attempts to give value to the undervalued, but the method he chooses to give people and causes value is that delineated here: he records places with tender attention to detail; he describes them closely and lists their attributes. We might argue that if politics is his subject, place is his theme.

Of course these are not separate entities, and Sean O'Brien's poetry is very much about finding points of fusion between them, but theme is what arises through subject, and O'Brien's themes are identifiable, not just by the care he takes to capture them, but by the air of bafflement and reverence they induce: 'these are not something to use but to enter, though I don't know why. They are sufficient.'

Activity 7.2   Writing

Take that first phrase from this piece: 'I want to write poems which . . .'
Write for 15–20 minutes a series of sentences all beginning with this
phrase. Allow yourself to range from grand themes ('I want to write
poems which are edible and thus solve world hunger'), to the apparently trivial ('I want to write poems containing corn on the cob'), even if
this causes you to suspect that not all your answers may be themes, or
even entirely true. The important thing with this exercise is to keep
going, to be writing down the rest of the sentence *almost* before
thinking.

The task here is to sort out the wheat from the chaff. Sometimes there
isn't any wheat, in which case you should set yourself this as a daily
exercise: five minutes before going to sleep or just after getting up.

Discussion

What you are looking for is the same thing you were looking for in the
first exercise in Chapter 1: a hook, something that catches your attention and niggles at you, so that you start wondering: 'Might that be
true?' One question you should certainly ask yourself is: 'Are these
potential themes reflected in anything I've actually written?' Sometimes
they are, but when they're not, perhaps you need to adjust your subject
matter.

Next time you go over your three lists – of favourite words, of titles and
of quotes – have a look at this list too: do you see any links, any possible
starting points?

Theme isn't something which you can impose on your writing; it's
something that writing imposes on you. Theme is that thing beyond our
present understanding which we embark on a piece of writing in the
hope of discovering. Often it can sneak up on you, so that you gradually
realise it's what you've already been writing about.

For years I supposed my writing was about recovering a sense of
intensity located in language and in places that I'd possessed as a
child, because I equated this with belonging somewhere, with being
acknowledged and being at home. Then it dawned on me that it was
precisely the intensity with which I experienced these things which meant
I didn't belong: it forced me out to a position where I can witness home
and endure lack of acknowledgement.

This version of my theme will probably mutate in another few years because, like writing, theme evolves, it isn't stable. People tend to look for hard-and-fast 'rules' that will carry them through the difficult business of being a writer. As I've said, there aren't any, but when you catch a glimpse of a pattern, it is, as O'Brien puts it, 'sufficient'.

Subject

Subject is to theme as the line is to the poem. It is that single coherent point of focus which nonetheless relates to something beyond itself. Most writers find in time that there is a certain range of subjects within which they write well, because these subjects enable them to express a key theme. This does not of course preclude the search for new ideas and new modes of expression. It just confirms that, with subject as with language, we emerge from a particular territory that shapes our tastes and interests. For some writers, this realisation begins a continually deepening search for the perfect expression of a given subject. For others it sets them on a quest for variations or even radically contrasting new subjects.

How we respond to a sense of our subject range can tell us a great deal about what kind of writer we are. There is of course always the danger of hardening into repetition, of making a virtue of limitation. But equally, there is always the possibility of growth, of continually more radical redefinition.

As we work with a sense of the greater body of our work, we confront the issue of ordering, of how to group subjects in order to engage the reader with the underlying themes.

Activity 7.3   Reading

Read 'Assumptions' by Richard Hugo, from *The Triggering Town*:

ASSUMPTIONS lie behind the work of all writers. The writer is unaware of most of them, and many of them are weird. Often the weirder the better. Words love the ridiculous areas of our minds. But silly or solid, assumptions are necessary elements in a successful base of writing operations. It is important that a poet not question his or her assumptions, at least not in the middle of composition. Finish the poem first, then worry, if you have to, about being right or sane.

Whenever I see a town that triggers whatever it is inside me that wants to write a poem, I assume at least one of the following:

The name of the town is significant and must appear in the title.

The inhabitants are natives and have lived there forever. I am the only stranger.

I have lived there all my life and should have left long ago but couldn't.

Although I am playing roles, on the surface I appear normal to the townspeople.

I am an outcast returned. Years ago the police told me to never come back but after all this time I assume that either I'll be forgiven or I will not be recognized.

At best, relationships are marginal. The inhabitants have little relation with each other and none with me.

The town is closely knit, and the community is pleasant. I am not a part of it but I am a happy observer.

A hermit lives on the outskirts in a one-room shack. He eats mostly fried potatoes. He spends hours looking at old faded photos. He has not spoken to anyone in years. Passing children often taunt him with songs and jokes.

Each Sunday, a little after 4 P.M., the sky turns a depressing gray and the air becomes chilly.

I run a hardware store and business is slow.

I run a bar and business is fair and constant.

I work in a warehouse on second shift. I am the only one in town on second shift.

I am the town humorist and people are glad to see me because they know I'll have some good new jokes and will tell them well.

[. . .]

On Saturday nights everyone has fun but me. I sit home alone and listen to the radio. I wish I could join the others though I enjoy feeling left out.

How concrete are his examples? Do you feel he's describing real circumstances, or scenes from a film?

Discussion

Notice how Hugo's description is as detailed as Sean O'Brien's. Almost everything is presented in concrete terms. And yet elements of this setting contradict each other: the composite nature of the triggering town, composed at once of many real and unreal towns, can quite happily contain contrary stimuli. The effect is both dream-like and cinematic, bobbing from grainy tracking shots to sudden documentary close-ups. It's not exactly a list of subjects, but it's certainly a list of those characteristics his potential subjects are likely to possess.

Because subject is a more objective area than theme, in that your work is always about something at a surface level, whereas theme may take several readings to emerge, it lends itself to these more graphic presentations. Can you tell from this list what Hugo's underlying theme is?

Notice the way he drifts in and out of the triggering town: sometimes he is present as a protagonist, sometimes he just records what's happening. Be aware that you may well be the subject of your poetry, but that doesn't mean it's all about you: other people, other voices, may define your subject as well as you do.

Activity 7.4   Writing

Look over everything you've written, the unfinished and less successful pieces as well as those you think might be starting to gel. Consider what you've been writing in your notebook. Everything is relevant at this stage. Take time to muse over all this – sleep on it and let your unconscious in on the process.

Then take 20 minutes to produce your own list of assumptions about your subject matter. As Hugo has done, don't go into why you're describing something, just describe it. You might be describing a particular place, as he does, or it may be a time of year or even an hour of the day, a particular point in someone's life – not necessarily your own.

Be detailed, evocative, persistent. Imagine you are a camera, or a journalist, or a tape recorder left whirring in a corner. Look at your subjects from close up; consider them through a telescope from sea.

Discussion

What did you get? Look for those areas of concern that chime with what you're actually writing and hold most promise in terms of what you want to write. By separating your subjects from your conscious motivation (why you think you're writing about them), you start to allow them an autonomous existence. Perhaps another motive will appear, perhaps even a motif, or a theme.

This is also a method of generating raw material. Are there any ideas here you could develop, by giving yourself 10 minutes to expand on something that you've just sketched out? The imagination has a remarkable capacity to put flesh on whichever bones you concentrate on.

Subject and theme are intimately interwoven: the more insight we possess into one, the more we can hope to possess into the other. The stronger a sense we have about those subjects which cause us the greatest creative excitement, the more definite we can be when embarking on a draft or a piece of reading – that this is our territory, somewhere we can thrive imaginatively.

We have to be alert to new subject areas when they are presented to us, and learning to identify that excitement can help us to distinguish between different possibilities. We can only test that, however, by being as open to new subjects as possible. It's only in the act of writing that we discover whether our intuition or lack of it was accurate.

Determining subject matter doesn't just affect the poems we might be going to write, it changes our attitude towards those we have already written. Pieces discovered to be within the area of our concerns become more central to any attempt to group our work and find an order.

Sequence

One of the difficulties writers often encounter arises from the attempt to completely cover a given subject in a single poem. Such poems can feel crammed and unfocused because there was an assumption that every aspect of that subject must be fitted in. The common perception that poetry is a pared-down art form can mean poets are reluctant to give themselves enough room to explore less predictable possibilities. The sequence is one way of allowing a subject to grow naturally.

By separating out different aspects of a subject and by trying different angles of approach, the sequence gives a writer a sense of perspective on how important a particular subject may be. It also provides insight into how poems interact with each other, a significant skill to develop as you move towards ordering large groupings.

Activity 7.5   Reading

Read 'Johann Joachim Quantz's Five Lessons' by W.S. Graham, from *New Collected Poems* (2004a: 228–31). Consider what the speaker's different subjects tell us about his student.

Johann Joachim Quantz's Five Lessons

The First Lesson

So that each person may quickly find that
Which particularly concerns him, certain metaphors
Convenient to us within the compass of this
Lesson are to be allowed. It is best I sit
Here where I am to speak on the other side
Of language. You, of course, in your own time
And incident (I speak in the small hours.)
Will listen from your side. I am very pleased
We have sought us out. No doubt you have read
My Flute Book. Come. The Guild clock's iron men
Are striking out their few deserted hours
And here from my high window Brueghel's winter
Locks the canal below. I blow my fingers.

The Second Lesson

Good morning, Karl. Sit down. I have been thinking
About your progress and my progress as one
Who teaches you, a young man with talent
And the rarer gift of application. I think
You must now be becoming a musician
Of a certain calibre. It is right maybe
That in our lessons now I should expect
Slight and very polite impatiences
To show in you. Karl, I think it is true
You are now nearly able to play the flute.

Now we must try higher, aware of the terrible
Shapes of silence sitting outside your ear
Anxious to define you and really love you.
Remember silence is curious about its opposite
Element which you shall learn to represent.

Enough of that. Now stand in the correct position
So that the wood of the floor will come up through you.
Stand, but not too stiff. Keep your elbows down.
Now take a simple breath and make me a shape
Of clear unchained started and finished tones.
Karl, as well as you are able, stop
Your fingers into the breathing apertures
And speak and make the cylinder delight us.

The Third Lesson

Karl, you are late. The traverse flute is not
A study to take lightly. I am cold waiting.
Put one piece of coal in the stove. This lesson
Shall not be prolonged. Right. Stand in your place.

Ready? Blow me a little ladder of sound
From a good stance so that you feel the heavy
Press of the floor coming up through you and
Keeping your pitch and tone in character.

Now that is something, Karl. You are getting on.
Unswell your head. One more piece of coal.
Go on now but remember it must be always
Easy and flowing. Light and shadow must
Be varied but be varied in your mind
Before you hear the eventual return sound.

Play me the dance you made for the barge-master.
Stop stop Karl. Play it as you first thought
Of it in the hot boat-kitchen. That is a pleasure
For me. I can see I am making you good.
Keep the stove red. Hand me the matches. Now
We can see better. Give me a shot at the pipe.
Karl, I can still put on a good flute-mouth
And show you in this high cold room something
You will be famous to have said you heard.

The Fourth Lesson

You are early this morning. What we have to do
Today is think of you as a little creator
After the big creator. And it can be argued
You are as necessary, even a composer
Composing in the flesh an attitude
To slay the ears of the gentry. Karl,
I know you find great joy in the great
Composers. But now you can put your lips to
The messages and blow them into sound
And enter and be there as well. You must
Be faithful to who you are speaking from
And yet it is all right. You will be there.

Take your coat off. Sit down. A glass of Bols
Will help us both. I think you are good enough
To not need me anymore. I think you know
You are not only an interpreter.
What you will do is always something else
And they will hear you simultaneously with
The Art you have been given to read. Karl,

I think the Spring is really coming at last.
I see the canal boys working. I realise
I have not asked you to play the flute today.
Come and look. Are the barges not moving?
You must forgive me. I am not myself today.
Be here on Thursday. When you come, bring
Me five herrings. Watch your fingers. Spring
Is apparent but it is still chilblain weather.

The Last Lesson

Dear Karl, this morning is our last lesson
I have been given the opportunity to
Live in a certain person's house and tutor
Him and his daughters on the traverse flute.
Karl, you will be all right. In those recent
Lessons my heart lifted to your playing.

I know. I see you doing well, invited
In a great chamber in front of the gentry. I
Can see them with their dresses settling in
And bored mouths beneath moustaches sizing
You up as you are, a lout from the canal
With big ears but an angel's tread on the flute.

But you will be all right. Stand in your place
Before them. Remember Johann. Begin with good
Nerve and decision. Do not intrude too much
Into the message you carry and put out.

One last thing Karl, remember when you enter
The joy of those quick high archipelagoes,
To make to keep your finger-stops as light
As feathers but definite. What can I say more?
Do not be sentimental or in your Art.
I will miss you. Do not expect applause.

Discussion

The first of these poems originally appeared in Graham's 1970 collection, *Malcolm Mooney's Land*. By his next book it had developed into a group of poems. When his *Collected Poems* appeared, Graham chose to present both forms: the single poem, and, later, the sequence. He evidently felt these were two quite different things. The style of the first poem is indeed less intimate than the rest, and, in the 'certain metaphors' we can see some of Graham's general themes – language and the difficulty of communication, darkness and its equation with silence and isolation.

When the poem appears by itself, the 'you' addressed in it can be regarded as general, a trope Graham often exploits to mean the reader is being addressed. When it's read as part of a sequence, the 'you' evolves into Karl, the student.

The principal effect Graham gains by writing in sequence is transition: an indeterminate but significant period of time elapses between each poem: Karl's skills develop, and his attitude towards his tutor shifts, from impatience through arrogance to humility, whereupon he can become Quantz's peer.

It won't have escaped you that this is the journey any writer takes in relation to his influences, but what Graham does, by emphasising the independence of the first poem, is suggest that this is also the journey undertaken by a reader in relation to understanding a poem. First they find it forbidding, then they run through Karl's responses, arriving at an understanding which makes them equal to the poem's creator. The reader creates the poem by reading it imaginatively: Graham presents the dynamics of this process.

What the rest of the sequence adds to the first poem is drama and detail: it allows it to be a narrative rather than only or primarily a metaphor for poetry. This allows for tonal contrast as the sequence shifts from the odd formality of 'I am very pleased/We have sought us out . . .' to the even colder austerity of:

> Now we must try higher, aware of the terrible
> Shapes of silence sitting outside your ear
> Anxious to define you and really love you.
> Remember silence is curious about its opposite
> Element which you shall learn to represent.

There is quirkiness in 'Unswell your head' and pathos as well as insight into genuine vocation in the conclusion: 'Do not be sentimental or in your Art./I will miss you. Do not expect applause.'

Activity 7.6 Writing

Look at the drafts you produced in response to the exercise on the muses in the chapter on voice. Consider whether or not you could revise these to create a sequence – nine short poems on contemporary meetings with the muses.

Perhaps you've already worked up your drafts for these. In that case, pick up the suggestion I made at the end of another exercise in the chapter on voice where I said to think of animals that resembled you. Select four animals: one to represent you as a child, one for you as a teenager, one as an adult, and one which represents you in old age. (You may need to predict one or more of these.) The animal can be a pet from that period, a creature you encountered then, or simply a beast, real or imaginary, which you feel sums up what kind of person you were or are or will be.

Write a poem about each of these four creatures, writing for 20 minutes on each over several days.

How did you write these poems? Were you present in them in some way, or did you depict the animals without much explanation? How little framing do you think they need? Did you take any formal decisions? Are the poems linked by their form or more diverse: how do they sit together in this sense?

Could any of them stand independently of the grouping? Are any less successful? (It wouldn't be terrible if you moved in the opposite direction to Graham, and came out of this with a single effective piece.) What is the progression of the sequence: do you feel the separate pieces add up to a kind of narrative, or are they simply a constellation, without any need to progress?

Do you feel any of the pieces you've worked on for this book ought to go together (even two poems makes a kind of sequence)?

When you write a sequence you're making a statement about the interdependence of the poems within it. You're saying that, whatever sense they make individually, they make a greater whole when put together. This can come from narrative drive, or expansion to provide greater detail. It can also be a matter of thematic binding. Some poems may need to be gathered under a single title. Graham's last book contains a sequence of seventy-odd pieces, some very short, under the same title as the collection: *Implements in Their Places* (2004b: 240–57).

The sequence is a sign that you've spread your wings a little, and want to move beyond the confines of the short lyric. This in itself is not necessarily a thing (think of your audience before writing 500 sonnets on trout flies), but it can mark a stronger grasp of subject and perhaps even theme. If you develop your formal skills alongside these, it can indicate that you are ready to mature.

Pamphlet

When we place poems together, whether in a reading folder or in a draft for a collection, it soon becomes apparent that they speak to each other. The space between poems can be as charged as the space between lines or stanzas within a single poem. There is an accumulated effect that we overlook by dipping into a book and picking out a single poem. This effect is not quite the same as a narrative, but it can give a similar sense of a developing atmosphere, supported or disrupted by each successive piece. A level on which to explore this effect is the pamphlet.

Pamphlets can consist of anything from around 12 to about 30 poems. They allow us to select and reject pieces, to space out main themes, to consider the dynamics of sub-sections or sequences, and to decide on opening and closing poems. Like individual poems, they require titles and possibly epigraphs, which makes us contemplate the most important impression we wish to give from this grouping of our work.

They mark a significant transition point in how we see and present our poetry.

Activity 7.7   Reading

Read Helen Dunmore, 'An unlikely ambition' in *How Poets Work*, ed. Tony Curtis (Bridgend: Seren, 1996:84). Compare this approach with how you read all the pieces you've produced so far.

> Another part of the process of writing poems which I have come to appreciate more and more is the first stage of writing a way into a poem, making marks which can be as crude as they need to be in order to define the territory of the poem. This primitive map-making is often shot through with one or two fully-formed phrases which embody the essential music of the poem, the sound which the ear follows and seeks to shape. So these early drafts may offer a startling contrast between writing which is done for the sake of getting somewhere else, and perfect fragments of the poem as it will become. As collections of poems develop, something similar happens on a large scale. At a certain point I realise not just that these poems are beginning to form a collection, but what kind of collection it is going to be. The poems talk to one another. There's an exchange of ideas, and an intricate web of language: touched at one point, it vibrates at another. I grow more and more interested in the shaping of the collection, and again there's the question of discarding work. A good poem may sit uneasily in a particular book, just as an image can be beautiful, but fail to function in a poem.

Discussion

Helen Dunmore neatly links the starting point and conclusion of this book on writing poetry: there is indeed a similarity between the way a draft develops into a poem, and how a group of poems evolves into a collection. The work you have done in this chapter on subject and theme should have started you on this process of, yet again, reading your own work, this time on the larger scale of assessing how poems might fit together.

Activity 7.8   Revising and ordering

You will already have begun the process of revising at least some of the pieces you have been asked to do in the exercises in Chapters 1–6. That process needs to be completed. Each exercise piece should be written up in the light of the work done across this course. That means considering each one in terms of its lineation and form, considering whether or not it should rhyme and in what way. Do any need to be gathered into a sequence? Are any still untitled? Would epigrams or footnotes enhance them?

Are there any suggestions I've made for other poems that you thought you could do something with? Have you made suggestions to yourself in your notebook about further pieces you could write? If so, you need to set aside composition time as well as time to revise. When is the best time for you to compose, and when should you revise?

Throughout this process consider order. If you have been able to isolate a theme then this may help you to focus: what are most of your poems about? Are there some which, as Helen Dunmore suggests, don't seem to fit with the others?

Try and create a spine of poems which go through the pamphlet, each one of which relates in some way to that central theme. These don't have to succeed each other directly: you can intersperse them with more miscellaneous ones. But if the reader keeps coming back to another poem on the same or a similar theme, then they will understand that there is a structure to the pamphlet, just as there is a form to individual pieces. If your sequence expresses your theme, then perhaps it could form a spine by itself: could it go in the middle?

Otherwise there's a simple pattern you could try: establish which poems you think are most successful – three will do – put one of these at the start of your pamphlet, one in the middle, and one at the end. This apparently cynical advice in fact imposes a rhythm on the whole group – not everything is going to be as good as everything else, so you might as well ensure that the peaks are in the right place. Then you can concentrate on making the troughs as shallow as possible.

Look at your titles and epigraphs. Is there one title, one epigraph which encapsulates your theme better or more pithily than others? Is this your pamphlet's title or will you have to invent another? Will this epigraph work or do you need another for the whole thing?

With titles it can be good to look inside poems as well as at their titles: sometimes there's a phrase or part of one which would work well. Look at your lists of quotes – here's how Edwin Morgan came up with one of his best titles:

> . . . the phrase actually came from a reviewer who had been look-ing at some of my poems and feeling that what I was doing was not so much variations on a theme, as it might seems on the surface to be, but rather the opposite – that it was really themes on a vari-ation. And when I read this, my ears seemed to prick up somehow, and although it was a strange sort of reversal I began to think about it and thought that there was probably some truth in it. It seemed to me that it did apply (although I didn't want to work it out) – I just liked the phrase.
>
> (Morgan 1990: 142)

Notice how, like Sean O'Brien with theme, he doesn't investigate too much what he likes about the title. This can be one of the great impedi-ments to completing any project: you may feel that you have to com-pletely understand every aspect of what you are doing before you let it go. This equates with re-revising a poem until all the life has been revised out of it. As Pope says: 'Whoever thinks a faultless piece to see/Thinks what ne'er was, nor is, nor e'er shall be.'

Both poets are determining instinctively when enough is enough. You must simply work as thoroughly and carefully on each poem and the collection as a whole as you have time. You're used to concentrating in bursts no longer than half an hour at a time. Not much will be gained by suddenly doubling or trebling this unit.

You've been asked to produce between 20 and 30 pieces of writ-ing. Not all of these are going to have yielded poems (though you should exert as much ingenuity as possible in order to turn them into poems). Nonetheless that's enough to generate a pamphlet-length group of work.

Be clear about the ones that don't fit because they're not good enough, or not finished, as well as those which stand out too much because of subject or theme – and leave them out. Be serious about ordering: a chronological sequence is tempting, but until you try to integrate them with each other, poems written in response to the different chapters may remain somewhat sealed off from each other.

By letting the poems speak to each other, you can integrate the work you've done. By revising each piece in the light of work done in the others, you can assess how far the different principles you've studied might integrate into your practice. By titling the whole group, you can try to reach some conclusions about theme, about what kind of writer you are at this point.

Luxuriate in the process of selection and ordering: shuffle your poems frequently and take pleasure in re-reading them. After the hard work you've done, you deserve to enjoy its results.

References

Dunmore, Helen (1996) 'An unlikely ambition', in Tony Curtis (ed.) *How Poets Work*. Bridgend: Seren.

Graham, W.S. (2004b) *Implements in Their Places*, in *New Collected Poems*, Matthew Francis (ed.). London: Faber and Faber.

Graham, W.S. (2004a) 'Johann Joachim Quantz's Five Lessons', in *New Collected Poems*, Matthew Francis (ed.). London: Faber and Faber.

Morgan, Edwin (1990) *Nothing Not Giving Messages: Reflections on work and life*, Hamish Whyte (ed.). Edinburgh: Polygon.

O'Brien, Sean (2000) 'Proceedings in Palmersville', in W.N. Herbert and Mathew Holl.

Part 2

Dialogue: Jo Shapcott (JS) and Bill Herbert (BH)

BH: Poems often seem to have a subject, but when you look at them a bit more that doesn't really seem to be what they're about in terms of theme, so you have got these kind of two layers going on. In your work frequently the case is that one reads something that seems to have quite a clear definite subject, a poem called 'Cabbages' or a poem about a particular scientific discovery, and if you try to read that poem just about that, then you learn one thing, but obviously there is something else going on as well. How do you think of these layers?

JS: I actually don't think of them in terms of theme and subject. Theme and subject take me back in a simple way to thinking, yes, subject, that is the title of the poem, shoes, tea trays, and that is what the poem is about, and maybe theme is something scattered among a lot of poems, but clearly that leaves so much out, doesn't it? I am aware that what is going on in one of my poems is just as much about a kind of image story, and maybe it is that which is guiding me through the poem, rather than what the ostensible subject is. In fact that is an idea that the Italian poet Cesare Pavese had: he talked about image narrative in reference to a poem of his that contained a hermit, and there is a line in the poem that compares the hermit to the colour of burnt bracken, and Pavese says about that that the poem is not about a hermit nor is it about bracken, but it is about the relationship between the two – and you start thinking about the relationship between hermit and nature.

BH: Is this one of the things which drives people nuts about poetry? They think, here is a poem, it is called something nice and straightforward, therefore it must be about something nice and straightforward – and then they just fall through a trapdoor into all the other things the poem is about.

JS: It is easy to forget that poets are readers too. I am an avid, keen reader of poetry; I find it exciting, and one of the exciting things is that you can take a poem called 'Cabbages' and read it at that level, and maybe find out a lot about cabbages and get quite excited about the music and the patterns in the poem, but you might dip into it again and you might find something different: you might notice there is something about the inner life, about dreams, secrets, aspirations as well, and then you start thinking about that strange relationship, that perhaps a bit surreal relationship, and you get shocked out of your normal way of thinking.

BH: I like what you are saying about theme as something that crops up here and there, almost like some kind of mushroom, a fungal growth, and how that relates to the idea of the image story – because we are not really talking about a narrative in consecutive plot-driven terms are we? We are talking about something that pervades something. So I am curious about how you become aware of that, how you first become aware you had a theme?

JS: That is a very difficult question because I think it happens at different stages in different poems, and that very often when you are at the point where you are putting together a book, you discover, looking back at your own work, new themes that you actually did not realise you put in there, but that are radiating out of the work very strongly, and might actually suggest a way of ordering the poems in that book to enhance the theme, to make the poems talk to each other.

BH: Writers often talk about discovering something through reading their own work; about something that happens, as you say, as you reach the end of a collection. This implies a state of tolerating, not knowing for quite a long time, what it is you are doing exactly.

JS: I think that is essential when trying to write a poem; I think it is absolutely the essence of it, that if through the active writing of the poem you do not discover something that you did not know you knew, or something fresh, then that poem is somehow dead. I think the reader also gets excited by the excitement that is contained in the poem from your discovery, and very often it is that image narrative that gives you that discovery; it is the resonances of the metaphors that you choose that you need to be alert to, because that is maybe telling you the real story of your poem. That is very useful actually, when revising: if you try and pick up how the images are working in your poem that can be the direction to nudge it gently rather than back to your title, 'Tea Trays' or 'The Lake in Snow' – whatever it is.

BH: So let's come back to the title for a moment: is it possible to argue that you embark on a subject – 'Tea Trays in the Snow' – but you discover a theme?

JS: That might be a good way of putting it. I checked out the origin of the words 'subject' and 'theme', and it is quite interesting: they both mean almost the same thing, one from Greek, one from Latin – they mean to put down or to place, but the difference may be 'subject' has got that 'sub' prefix which means 'down', that theme does not have. So maybe the subject is the place where you put the theme: theme maybe lives inside the subject but is more than the subject, which is like its house.

BH: Sometimes in your work there is quite a clear sequence of thematic grouping, which comes from say the translation, the adaptation – it is a group and it is discrete, but in other cases, and I am thinking for instance about the mad cow poems, there is almost a sequence there, but it is scattered, it crops up here and there across books. Why is there a difference of that kind and how do you think the reader puts those things together?

JS: I think writers get obsessions and they don't go away, so those ideas might be living with you for many years, but, just as if you take Van Gogh's sunflowers, he is not painting lots of sunflowers because he has run out of ideas, he is painting lots of sunflowers because he wants to explore light and shade and how they operate in different ways with perhaps the same material. I think maybe that is what obsession is: you return to it to discover something new, almost coming at it from lots and lots of different angles as if only that way can you get to the truth. I read a bit of really mad but interesting research on Darwin and some other creative thinkers: it was about Darwin's notebooks and the research maintained that actually there are very few recurring big ideas in the notebooks and they are meta-phorical ideas, for example branching was one of the main themes, if you like, that came up in Darwin's early notebooks – and if you think about it, branching prefigures the whole idea of evolution. So by repeating to himself this idea of branching and flowering in lots of different ways, he was consolidating a brilliant huge idea. You can see that in Leonardo De Vinci too: if you look at his notebooks you will follow the idea of a spiral through the spiral in a leaf pattern, in water, in waves, in clouds, and he will write about it, he will sketch it, every medium, every kind of spiral he can see, and he won't let go until he feels he has looked at it from every single angle and in every possible way.

BH: I begin to understand the image story when you give these instances, because these are people who are thinking of things in metaphorical patterns, in terms of how one piece of information leads to another way of working. It is not narrative, though, is it? It is sort of analogical, it is almost transformative?

JS: I think that is absolutely right. When we think of metaphor we often think of it, I think wrongly, as parallels, so a cloud is like a tea tray – there is a kind of parallel there, but I think it would be truer to say there is relationship and there is a connection of actually like and not like, and that is exciting. I think there is a frisson about a metaphor and the subject from which it originates that is always very thrilling because of the likeness and the non-likeness.

BH: Is this how you begin to suspect that you are writing a sequence when you get these thrills, these moments? How do you recognise that that is what you are now doing?

JS: Well, I have got about nine or ten poems written in the voice of a mad cow, and I only ever intended her to have one single poem. She stayed with me; she got lots and lots, and I think it is that idea that there was more to say, that in a way it is writing the same poem, but it is from different angles, and that somehow, in order to get the whole experience, the whole idea, you need more than one shot at it. (see Activity 3.5, p. 63)

I don't think you always know the theme at the time of writing the poem. It wasn't until I put together a couple of connections that I realised they were peopled with humans and creatures that were constantly falling over – cartoon characters that fell over, a mad cow who fell over – and I thought that through a little bit and realised I was interested in things that were literally fallible rather than perfect, and that has since become something I have more consciously adopted as an idea.

BH: How much do you need to be conscious of these processes? Coming back to people who are beginning to write and who are beginning to think, 'Shall I write two poems on this theme or should I just try and get it all into one poem?' There is a question about how much you need to be aware in order to make these decisions.

JS: I think you can't be totally aware, because something happens at the end of the process of you writing the poem, and that is that you give it to a reader, and you won't know everything that reader knows, the reader is going to bring a whole lot of other experiences and ideas to your poem, and discover things in it that are certainly there because of your life experience and your knowledge, but you did not necessarily consciously put there. I have got a little poem called 'Goat', which is ostensibly about a goat, in which the speaker undergoes a metamorphosis rather like that green guy who changes into the Hulk, so this happens in my poem, but when I read it at a reading, people often come up and talk to me about it and they will say, 'You know you read that poem "Goat"? Well, that was actually about greed wasn't it?' And I will say, 'Oh, yes, um, um.' Or 'that was actually about consumerism', and I go, 'Well that is really interesting, yeah.' Or most often they will say, 'That poem, "Goat", that was about men, don't you think?' They are right, and it is very exciting for them to pick out for you some of the processes that you have brought to your poem.

Goat

Dusk, deserted road, and suddenly
I was a goat. To be truthful, it took
two minutes, though it seemed sudden,
for the horns to pop out of my skull,
for the spine to revolutionise and go
horizontal, for the fingers to glue
together and for the nails to become
important enough to upgrade to hoof.
The road was not deserted anymore, but full
of goats, and I liked that, even though I hate
the rush hour on the tube, the press of bodies.
Now I loved snuffling behind his or her ear,
licking a flank or two, licking and snuffling here,
there, wherever I liked. I lived for the push
of goat muscle and goat bone, the smell of goat fur,
goat breath and goat sex. I ended up on the edge
of the crowd where the road met the high
hedgerow with the scent of earth, a thousand
kinds of grass, leaves and twigs, flower-heads
and the intoxicating tang of the odd ring-pull
or rubber to spice the mixture. I wanted
to eat everything. I could have eaten the world
and closed my eyes to nibble at the high
sweet leaves against the sunset. I tasted
that old sun and the few dark clouds
and some tall buildings far away in the next town.
I think I must have swallowed an office block
because this grinding enormous digestion tells me
it's stuck on an empty corridor which has
at the far end, I know, a tiny human figure.

BH: There is a nice idea in what you say that one ostensible subject may have many themes, and that is one of the great delights of a poem, that it can be reread in so many ways and that some of these will mean more to you as a writer than others, and that is a learning process that you embark on. Now when that becomes most conscious, you were suggesting that it is when you get to the end of a process, and if that process were writing a sequence or writing a collection, how does that relate to how you would then order the collection, is there a narrative that you are trying to establish at that point?

JS: There is, and I think it is actually happening more and more in contemporary poetry, there is a lot of attention paid to how the book is laid out, in what order the poems come, which I think is relatively new. Even when I published my first book in the 1980s there wasn't so much attention to that – my poems just went in chronologically. But now it is almost like writing another poem on a bigger scale. And you do find that they resonate and speak to each other, and you can group them if you like to intensify a certain theme that you have discovered that you would like the reader to feel at their fingertips when they are reading.

BH: A lot of people do get very caught up in the finish of the individual poem and it is salutary to think that this poem is talking to another poem and to another poem, and all of these poems which you have written may indeed be in conversation with each other, and there may be a way of ordering that will bring that into a kind of harmony. We skirted around the words 'narrative' and 'story' a couple of times, but this seems to be a different way of ordering than a story or a plot, nonetheless it does have a kind of geography to it, there is a kind of sense of a territory being laid out, and these things are within this territory and if the reader finds them, or if the reader finds them in an order even, then that enhances the experience of just reading a single poem and it starts to mean that they are reading the whole book.

JS: I think that is a really exciting thing about picking up that slim book of poems, that you have got more than one experience if you like: you have that experience of reading the poem and inhabiting that world – and I think each poem is its own world – but then you have got the larger experience of inhabiting the world that is the whole book and wandering through it, going back to it, getting to know it and then feeling the poems as they relate to each other. It is almost two different experiences but both are ones that you want and you can enhance and bring them out. There is a downside to that as well for the writer anyway which is that poems in a sequence are often forgotten as individual poems. You may think Poem Three on the tea tray was the best thing you ever wrote, but it will really never be seen outside its sequence, and that sometimes makes me sad when I wave goodbye to poems and send them off in their book.

BH: When we talked about subject it seemed like that was potentially something that was like a title, it was something quite straight-forward, it was a definition almost. I think some people sometimes worry that if theme exists in their writing, it ought to be similarly definite, almost an abstraction like their theme is Englishness, their theme is – you mentioned the body – but that it is a very definite thing. I get the impression the theme is much more a shifting, a matter of process. You can have a whole set of dialogues with yourself as you develop as a writer. Are you aware that these kind of hard abstractions emerge as themes or do you think there is another way of looking at that?

JS: I think it has got to be more fluid than that; that you may have written several poems which to others it would be apparent have a strong theme and not recognise it for a while, and then realise that's something of interest to you and then consciously develop it. The American poet Charles Simic did something very interesting that I think shed some light on this. Early on in his career he wrote some very short simple lyrics ostensibly about very basic objects like stone, shoes, fork, knife, in which he miraculously makes these objects resonate beyond themselves. Again, I think it is the relationship between the objects he chose and all the other things it makes you think of, that become the subject of the poem.

BH: We have been talking about these rather clear things and trying to define them 'subject', 'theme' and sometimes we found the def-initions are not necessarily as clear, but do you ever think about these matters when you are writing a poem?

JS: I think you probably don't. In the end I suspect you hope your reader won't be consciously driving themselves to think about them either when they are reading that poem. We have talked about a poem in terms of it being a world of its own and just like the world it has got so many different aspects to it which is to do with its music, the way that it appeals to you beyond your conscious level as a reader, and I think all those things operate. Themes help that but themes are not the whole story, they are only part of it.

BH: They are nice little props which we must really knock down as we proceed further into the world of the poem?

JS: Definitely. I think the experience of the reader should be much more organic. More than that: in the end, if the poem is going to work, it is about something more than itself, it is about something more than its ostensible subject, it is about more than the themes and that is something that's maybe unsayable in the end, it may be to do with the spirit, God, imagination.

BH: So just very strictly in terms of the writing process, this is something which comes up at stages in the writing process, but it certainly does not sound like it is something you should set out on a little piece of paper before you write the poem?

JS: Definitely not. I think you must try and discover something through the poem that you did not know you knew and if you have it all planned out like that, if you have got it mapped, then you are going to get lost in an ironic kind of way, you will be lost.

BH: So drawing the map is the best way of getting lost?

JS: Yes, exactly. This is from a sequence of poems all about roses. There are about 20 of them and each one has the name of a different rose in botanical Latin and you need to think about roses, love, femininity, because I think as a whole the group makes one big love poem, although it is about 20 different little roses.

Rosa Gallica
If sometimes you're surprised
by my coolness
it's because inside myself,
petal against petal, I'm asleep.

I've been completely awake while my heart
dozed, for who knows how long,
speaking aphids and bees to you in silence,
speaking English through a French mouth.

You can see these poems as being in conversation with a set of poems also called 'The Roses' written by the poet Rainer Maria Rilke. His roses are rather different, though. In his poems he addresses them and he tells them what it is like to be them, he is describing it on their behalf. His roses aren't named and mine are, and there is a kind of argument if you look at the poems side by side, in which he says it is like this and my poems say back no, it is not, it is like this.

> **Rosa Hemispherica**
> You see me as half-open,
> a book whose pages
> can be turned by the wind
> then read with your eyes closed;
>
> butterflies stream out,
> stunned to discover
> they think just like you,
> dab wings all over your face.

Unlike more organic fluid sequences that I have written like the one involving the mad cow which was completely open and just took me anywhere that it led me, 'The Roses' in a way is more schematic because it is this conversation with the poems of Rilke, so in that sense each person answers one of his poems and the whole idea is limited and enclosed in that way. Although mine spin out in such a different way that I still think of it as one huge love poem, maybe a love poem to Rilke himself.

> **Rosa Sancta**
> Now you've made
> a saint out of me,
> Saint Rose, open-handed,
> she who smells of God naked.
>
> But, for myself, I've learned
> to love the whiff of mildew
> because though not Eve, exactly,
> yes, I stink of the Fall.

References

Shapcott, Jo (1992) 'Goat', in *Phrase Book*. Oxford: Oxford Poets, p.11.
Shapcott, Jo (1998) 'Les Roses', in *My Life Asleep*. Oxford: Oxford University Press, p. 30; p. 34.

Index

187

Index of first lines